January–April 2015

Rooting women's lives in the Bible

Christina Press
BRF
Tunbridge Wells/Abingdon

First published in Great Britain 2015

ISBN 978 0 85746 125 4

Distributed in Australia by:
Mediacom Education Inc., PO Box 610, Unley, SA 5061.
Tel: 1800 811 311; Fax: 08 8297 8719;
E-mail: admin@mediacom.org.au

Distributed in New Zealand by:
Scripture Union Wholesale, PO Box 760, Wellington
Tel: 04 385 0421; Fax: 04 384 3990;
E-mail: suwholesale@clear.net.nz

Acknowledgments

Scripture quotations taken from The Holy Bible, New International Version (Anglicised edition), copyright © 1979, 1984, 2011 by Biblica. Used by permission of Hodder & Stoughton Publishers, an Hachette UK company. All rights reserved. 'NIV' is a registered trademark of Biblica. UK trademark number 1448790.

Scripture quotations taken from The Holy Bible, Today's New International Version, copyright © 2004 by Biblica. Used by permission of Hodder & Stoughton Publishers, an Hachette UK company. All rights reserved. 'TNIV' is a registered trademark of Biblica.

Scripture quotations taken from The New Revised Standard Version of the Bible, Anglicised Edition, copyright © 1989, 1995 by the Division of Christian Education of the National Council of the Churches of Christ in the United States of America, are used by permission. All rights reserved.

Scripture quotations from THE MESSAGE. Copyright © by Eugene H. Peterson 1993, 1994, 1995. Used by permission of NavPress Publishing Group.

Scripture quotations from the Holy Bible, New Living Translation, copyright © 1996, 2004. Used by permission of Tyndale House Publishers, Inc., Wheaton, Illinois 60189. All rights reserved.

Scripture quotations taken from the New King James Version of the Bible copyright © 1979, 1980, 1982 by Thomas Nelson, Inc. All rights reserved.

Printed by Gutenberg Press, Tarxien, Malta.

Contents

Contributors

Sandra Wheatley remains as active as possible, despite the constraints of MS and a wheelchair. She enjoys an extensive prayer ministry and has mastered swimming and praying at the same time.

Katy Jack, a lawyer by trade, is a mother of three young boys and supports her husband's ministry as chaplain in a boarding school. She loves netball and camping holidays.

Claire Musters is a freelance writer and editor, mum to two young children, pastor's wife, worship leader and school governor. Claire's writing focuses on marriage, parenting, worship, discipleship and issues facing women today.

Alison Teale works as an administrator in tertiary education and has worked as a freelance writer and translator for 20 years.

Annie Kirke is an ordained pioneer priest in the Diocese of London. She trains and teaches on developing missional communities in London, discipling 20s and 30s, and inner healing prayer.

Jill Rattle is a former secondary head teacher and, for some years, was involved in selecting candidates for ordination training and for naval officer training. She now exercises a ministry to individuals seeking spiritual direction.

Jean Watson is a writer, spiritual director and trustee of a local counselling service. Her work has included teaching, editing and writing for children and adults, and her articles, stories and scripts have been published in books and magazines and used on radio and TV.

Bola Adamolekun is a huge fan of dark chocolate and speculative fiction. She loves playing badminton and dancing at her favourite club. She is also a writer, a potter and a Church of England ordinand.

Amy Boucher Pye is a writer, speaker and editor living in north London. She runs the *Woman Alive* book club and is writing her first book. An American by birth, she delights in all things British, especially her husband and children.

Chris Leonard lives in Surrey with her husband. With two children now married, she remains busy leading creative writing courses and holidays. Her 20th book was published in August 2013.

Christine Platt lives in New Zealand and travels regularly with teams to East Timor to support the church there in its courageous witness to war-ravaged people. She writes Bible studies and devotional notes in the Tetun language.

Ali Herbert writes...

It is a great pleasure for me to bring you this issue of *Day by Day with God* at the start of 2015!

It's my privilege to take over as Editor from Catherine Butcher, who has edited these notes for the last decade. Many of us have had our spiritual lives enriched and our journey encouraged because of the thought and prayer that Catherine has poured into these notes over the years, and I should like to thank and honour Catherine for her hard work and for following God's guiding throughout. There was a special moment for me some months back when Catherine and I met for our 'handover'. As we prayed, we had a sense of 'passing on the baton', which is exciting and, of course, daunting in equal measure. It was quite an emotional moment for us both—very often the case as one season ends and a new season begins.

That brings us to this new season of 2015 and the knowledge of leaving the 'old' behind and pressing on into the new. To be honest, some of us will be relieved to have left 2014 behind, with its struggles and painful memories, and others will already be feeling nostalgic. Whichever it is for you, the world continues to turn at 1040 miles an hour (and it feels like it sometimes!) and we can be encouraged that, whatever this year brings, God remains the same: ready to welcome us into his presence and to do the new things he promises. As he says in Revelation, 'I am making everything new!' and what a relief and joy it is to know that he continues to do that in our lives!

The overall theme of these notes is 'Living life to the full'—the wonderful promise that Jesus has for us. Whether we are looking at the Psalms or the life of Miriam, the wisdom in Proverbs or the encouragement in 2 Timothy, we see a message from all sides that God is for us and with us, and that he longs for us to know a fullness of life in him. In this new year I am praying that we will each know more and more of the life of Jesus and the power of his Spirit in us.

So may I wish you a happy—and life-filled—brand new year!

The breath of life

The Lord God formed a man from the dust of the ground and breathed into his nostrils the breath of life, and the man became a living being.

Happy New Year! We have made it into another brand new year with all its potential and possibilities. My new years, of late, have often started where the old year left off, with busyness to contend with and lots of loose ends to tie up from the old year before embarking on the new, and that busyness so often brings me close to exhaustion. What a wonderful opportunity there is today to catch my breath and to be reminded just where that 'breath' originates.

I love reading the creation story; it sits comfortably with me as I delight in God's workmanship and his attention to detail. The pinnacle of creation, as has often been said, is you and me. Every other aspect of creation was spoken into being, but the man was fashioned by God, who got down amid the dust and dirt and formed him with his own bare hands. He was a wonderful combination of dust and deity, but God wasn't content with just the form of a man. God breathed life into him, and our unique relationship with God began.

At the start of this new year, it has been good for me to ponder on that moment in the creation story. I know that this little lump of dust and dirt is in need of God's breath once again—his life filling mine, his hands fashioning me and preparing me for all that lies ahead.

I need not only to catch my breath after the busyness of all that has passed but also to catch *his* breath and be renewed and restored. His breath brings life once again to my dusty dry life. It sounds so simple, doesn't it? But, of course, breathing is simple.

'Breathe on me, breath of God; fill me with life anew.'

SANDRA WHEATLEY

The meaning of life

'I have come that they may have life, and have it to the full.'

This little snippet of a verse has echoed throughout my Christian life since I was eleven years old. When I asked Jesus into my heart and life, the transformation was instantaneous: I wasn't just born again; I felt as if I'd been 'launched'. The church I attended was a new and lively charismatic one, independent of any other structure or organisation. Its freedom often went beyond the liberty in worship that we experienced and included a 'freedom' in interpreting the scriptures that, with hindsight, causes me some concerns and a wry smile.

John 10:10 was often used as a quantitative goal rather than a qualitative aim. I remember trying so hard to understand why some people around me were striving for the abundance of *things*: they saw these objects as evidence of the abundant life that Jesus promised. For me, though, it wasn't happening that way: life was becoming a struggle.

I asked God to help me to understand. He did, and I learned that it was the breath of God that brought life. All I needed to know was how to allow that truth to grow in my life.

There are two words for life in Greek—*bios*, from which we derive the word 'biology', and *zoe*, which means spiritual life. *Bios* life is the life that comes to us from nature—the life that always tends to run down and decay and needs to be nourished constantly with air, water and food. Spiritual life, on the other hand, is the life that is in God from all eternity, which has always existed and will always exist.

If someone promised to give us money 'abundantly', we would immediately understand that they meant 'lots' of money. Perhaps Jesus came, then, to give us 'lots of life'. Lord Jesus, how I need 'lots of life' today!

SANDRA WHEATLEY

A new life

I have been crucified with Christ... The life I now live in the body, I live by faith in the Son of God, who loved me and gave himself for me.

To move from Jesus' wonderful promise of 'life to the full' to today's reading about crucifixion may seem to be quite a big leap, but a peek at John 10:11 gives us a clue as to the radical message and the personal example that Jesus brought. The life Jesus imparts is no ordinary life, no ordinary existence. Once we have experienced it, we are changed for ever. At times, the mysteries of it elude and mystify us, and that's what I love about it.

Having given us this life, what does Jesus ask us to do with it? Live it up or lay it down? In Matthew 16:24–27 Jesus leaves his disciples (including us) in no doubt about the requirements of the life he imparts.

As I read through the epistles and settled on today's reading, it seemed to me that Paul identified with the experience of being crucified. Somehow he managed to make the subtle shift from the life he wanted to the life he chose to live, in being willing to 'die to self and live for God'.

That seems a good place to stop for a moment, to ponder these things before we embark upon reading some of Jesus' incredible encounters with people just like you and me. As we draw alongside Paul today, may we see that Jesus asked us to live and die for him, just as he died and lives for us. We are 'living sacrifices', aware that in Christ we have 'died' and yet are more alive than ever before.

Once again, Lord, help us to lay down what we cannot keep, and take hold of what we cannot lose—new life in you. Amen

SANDRA WHEATLEY

A searching life

Now there was a Pharisee, a man named Nicodemus who was a member of the Jewish ruling council. He came to Jesus at night and said, 'Rabbi, we know that you are a teacher who has come from God.'

The opening chapters of John's Gospel are full of interactions between Jesus and individuals, and they show the amazing impact he had on them.

Jesus' meeting with Nicodemus is intriguing. Nicodemus may have been among the group of Pharisees who questioned John the Baptist, in John 1:25. He may have been present when Jesus cleared the temple (2:12–25); if not, he would certainly have heard about it, as he was a member of the Sanhedrin. Now he seeks Jesus out on his own—in the dark, in every sense of the word.

We can sometimes forget that even among the Pharisees of Jesus' day, some will have had hearts seeking for 'something more'. I have a feeling that something stirred in Nicodemus' life as he and Jesus talked. Just as Jesus spoke of the wind blowing wherever it pleases, I wonder if there was a gentle breeze in Nicodemus' heart—the desire to know what it was to be 'born again'.

For many Christians, the 'born again' experience is vivid: the date and time of their 'new birth' are as important as the date and time of their physical birth. For others, although they may not have had that experience, their faith is just as real and their life in Jesus just as vital. There is no record that Nicodemus was 'born again' but he does speak up for Jesus later in John's Gospel (7:50–51) and is mentioned again when he and Joseph of Arimathea take Jesus' body from the cross and lay it in Joseph's tomb (19:39).

Something stirred in Nicodemus' life on the night when he sought Jesus out and heard him speak of new life, eternal life, kingdom life. This is the life that Jesus still gives to you and me, now and for ever.

Lord Jesus, may my heart be always seeking more of you. Whenever I seek you, in the daytime or the night, may I find you waiting. Amen
                                                                    SANDRA WHEATLEY

A thirsty life

Jesus answered, 'Everyone who drinks this water will be thirsty
again, but whoever drinks the water I give them will never thirst.
Indeed, the water I give them will become in them a spring of
water welling up to eternal life.'

Another day in Jesus' life and another remarkable encounter! This time
it is in the heat of the day, with a woman who had a thirsty life. Many
of us will have read this familiar story of the woman at the well, identified with it and been thankful that it is included in the scriptures as a
wonderful illustration of Jesus once again going against convention and
transforming a life—a needy life, just like our own.
  There are so many aspects of the story that strike me: all of the disciples had gone to buy food (it took twelve men to do the shopping!);
Jesus was bone-achingly tired and thirsty; he needed someone to help
him; he knew that the approaching woman had a greater thirst than
his. The scene was set for another remarkable one-to-one encounter,
just as in yesterday's reading, that would transform a life and satisfy a
thirst.
  I wonder what the day holds for you. Are you longing for Jesus to
satisfy that nagging thirst in your life, or are you going to be on the
look-out for some thirsty soul who could be encouraged by your new
life in Jesus?
  I have a wonderful friend called Duncan. He is a natural evangelist:
wherever he goes and whatever he is doing, he strikes up a conversation
with someone alongside him on the train or standing in the queue at
the bank or in a supermarket. Quick as a flash, he introduces references
to faith and spirituality and, with incredible regularity, names and contact details are exchanged and Duncan is organising a Bible study with
his new friend. He often texts me to ask me to pray, and I smile. Duncan reminds me of Jesus with this woman at the well.

---

*Lord Jesus, whatever I do and whoever I encounter today, may my thirst
be quenched or may I pour out to others the water of life that I receive
from you. Amen*

SANDRA WHEATLEY

A waiting life

One who was there had been an invalid for thirty-eight years.

Jesus went to Jerusalem to celebrate one of the Jewish feasts, but, rather than going to the temple, he went to the Sheep Gate and walked through to the Pool of Bethesda, also known as the House of Mercy. What confronted him was not only the pool for washing and cleaning the sheep before they were sacrificed at the temple but also a veritable sea of humanity, desperate for help and healing. These people were waiting and watching for the waters of the pool to be 'stirred' so that the first one in could be healed. You can almost feel and smell (wet sheep aren't the most aromatic!) the desperation that hung over the place—until into it all stepped Jesus.

I have no idea why Jesus singled out just one man, a man who had waited 38 years for healing to come. He'd been waiting at the pool even before Jesus was born—waiting and watching.

Some are born to wait; others have waiting thrust upon them, and then there are those who achieve the ability to wait simply because there is little else that they can do. Perhaps that is how you feel; perhaps a yearning for change or healing has loomed over you again today and you're feeling the weight of the waiting.

Today's reading gives us hope. There is always hope that our time will come and Jesus will heal our hurts, mend our brokenness and restore our bodies, even after 38 years or more of waiting. The stirring you see or feel isn't in a pool; it is in your heart, and today could be the day Jesus draws alongside. As I type these words, I'm praying that you will feel his presence and know his healing and wholeness.

If you can take some time to be still, to wait for the 'stirring of the waters', this could be your day, your time!

SANDRA WHEATLEY

A sinful life

The Pharisees… made her stand before the group and said to Jesus, 'Teacher, this woman was caught in the act of adultery. In the Law Moses commanded us to stone such women. Now what do you say?'

It must have been quite an entrance—the kerfuffle, the noise, the anger and the screams from the woman. The scene is set for another remarkable 'life-on-life' encounter. This time a woman's life hangs in the balance. There is no doubt that she is guilty—she was 'caught in the act of adultery'—but now we see Jesus caught in the act of compassion.

John makes it clear that the scribes and Pharisees are setting Jesus up (at this woman's expense), but Jesus knows it. In stooping down, he isn't ducking the issue but is perhaps letting accused and accusers see one another for what they are. Maybe we like to think that sins like this one are hidden and out of view. Adultery is a serious act—but then the sins I have committed are no less serious and sometimes I'd rather they were hidden, too.

We're probably capable of playing the part of both accuser and accused in this story. Sometimes we take a lofty view of those around us, those 'caught in the act' whose wrongdoings make us feel momentarily good about ourselves. But we all stand before Jesus, exposed and vulnerable, dishevelled in our sin, guilty as charged. Nothing is hidden from him. He knows the depth of our guilt—the shame and remorse. The stones of justice could rain down on us, but they don't. Instead, his mercy comes to us; his forgiveness follows and our lives are made free from the sin that haunts us, hamstrings us and condemns us.

Jesus said, 'Go now and leave your life of sin' (v. 11). He gave the woman permission—and a commission—to 'go', just as he gave it to his disciples in Matthew 28:19. She was free to live in him and because of him.

Lord Jesus, you have transformed my sinful life into a new life. Keep me always mindful that it is through your death that I live. Thank you.
SANDRA WHEATLEY

From death to life

'Lord,' Martha said to Jesus, 'If you had been here, my brother would not have died. But I know that even now God will give you whatever you ask.'

There is no greater contrast in scripture than John chapters 10 and 11. Jesus' promise of 'life to the full' can seem a million miles away from the story of Lazarus' death, yet the impact of Jesus' life on others and the life he gives are borne out in this story.

Jesus' friend, Lazarus, was ill. Lazarus' sisters, Mary and Martha, had sent word to Jesus, and then they waited and watched… and waited. Four days after Lazarus' death, Jesus came to them.

I don't understand the whys and wherefores of this story. Of course, the story of Lazarus' resurrection is an incredible one, but how many times has this scene been played out in millions of lives—in your life and mine, when we have asked the Lord to come? We have waited for him to come, watched as something or even someone precious to us has died, and tried not to let our hope and faith die, too. There are so many things I don't understand, these days, but one thing I do know. One thing has happened time and again for me, though perhaps not at the moment I've wanted or demanded it: Jesus has come.

Sometimes, like Martha, I've got into a discussion with him about how easier my life would have been if he had only healed me or changed the situation. But more often than not, all I've been able to do is to fall at his feet and weep—and know that he has wept with me.

Just as Jesus didn't stop there with Mary or Martha, but took them on to see the most incredible miracle happen, he has taken me on, too. He has taken me to places with him where 'resurrection' has come, and renewed hope and strength to carry on. Jesus' new life has filled this battered and bruised one.

Two little words spoken by Martha encourage and challenge me: 'even now'. Can I have the same faith in Jesus, saying, 'Even now I trust you, Lord'?

SANDRA WHEATLEY

A thankful life

Six days before the Passover, Jesus came to Bethany, where
Lazarus lived, whom Jesus had raised from the dead. Here a dinner
was given in Jesus' honour.

It seems that every Hollywood blockbuster these days must have a
sequel. We're gripped by a storyline and we're drawn in to its continu-
ation. Could today's reading be entitled 'Raised from the Dead Part 2'?

Just a few weeks after the dramatic events of Lazarus' death and resurrection, the plot to kill Jesus has intensified and the Pharisees have
decided that Lazarus should be included in it too. Jesus hasn't been
able to move around freely since raising Lazarus, but six days before the
Passover and his death, he is invited to a meal in his honour with his
friends in Bethany.

Martha serves the meal; Lazarus is 'with him', reclining at the table
and bearing testimony to the miraculous work of God in his life; Mary
is at Jesus' feet, poised with her expensive perfume, about to perform
an incredible act of devotion. All three form part of our Christian experience—worship, service and bearing testimony to what Jesus has done
for us. The impact on these three people's lives had been immense.
They all knew what Jesus meant when he said, 'I have come that they
might have life'.

We too have an opportunity every day of our lives to worship, to
serve and to share the good news. We may feel more comfortable in
serving than sharing. We may just want to give our all at Jesus' feet
and lavish our love and devotion on him. Whatever it is today that you
feel drawn to do, just do it, and enjoy every aspect of it. Don't fear the
detractors who may look on and ask, 'Why this waste?' (v. 5). You've
been made alive in Jesus by his death and resurrection. Let him know
and let others see all that he has done and all that he means to you.

---

*My precious Saviour, I worship you with my whole heart and mind and
life today. I love you, Jesus. Amen*

SANDRA WHEATLEY

Eternal life

'Now this is eternal life: that they know you, the only true God, and Jesus Christ, whom you have sent.'

'To know him': that desire sums up my life. In any and every circumstance, good or bad, I want to know him. Eternal life isn't a far-off hope; it is a present-day reality. From the moment I asked Jesus into my heart and life, eternal life commenced. In present-day parlance, I'm 'living the dream'!

Some years ago, when my ability to 'do' was lessening and all I could do was 'be', my heart was stirred by this scripture and I began a journey into intimacy with God that has been both profound and precious. I love the little wordplay that makes 'intimacy' mean 'Into me see'. This kind of knowledge is a huge risk for many of us. We're more used to keeping our lives safe and closed. If God were really to see into us, he really wouldn't like us—that's what I used to fear.

But knowing him and being known by him is the most life-changing experience we can have. The gentleness of his gaze, the tenderness of his presence and the comfort of his touch are ours, now and always.

I wonder if, at the start of this new year, you have been given this edition of *Day by Day with God* as a Christmas gift. You may not even have taken the first tentative step towards Jesus, asking him into your life, or you may be feeling that the steps you have taken have slowed down and you're floundering in your faith. As I write, I wonder if you need to ask Jesus to give you the life that had such an impact on the people we've been reading about, over these past days. You may be seeking life; you may be in the midst of a thirsty life or a sinful life or just longing for life. If you are, then this prayer might help.

Lord, I long to know you, the only true God, and Jesus Christ, whom you have sent. Come into my life, Lord Jesus.

SANDRA WHEATLEY

Making links

Katy Jack writes:

If you could ask God for one thing and you knew you would get it, what would you ask for? What would you really love the Lord to give you right now?

Well, that was the question young King Solomon had to answer shortly after he came to the throne of his father, King David. You can read the account in 1 Kings 3. The Lord appeared to Solomon during the night and said to him, 'Ask for whatever you want me to give you.' Solomon didn't ask for wealth, power or territories. He humbly acknowledged his need for wisdom. He saw the task of governing Israel stretching before him and so he asked the Lord to give him 'a discerning heart to govern [God's] people and to distinguish between right and wrong' (1 Kings 3:9). God was pleased with his request and promised to give him 'a wise and discerning heart, so that there will never have been anyone like you, nor will there ever be' (v. 12). What a promise!

God (unsurprisingly!) keeps his promise. In 1 Kings 4 we are told that 'God gave Solomon wisdom and very great insight, and a breadth of understanding as measureless as the sand on the seashore. From all nations people came to listen to Solomon's wisdom' (vv. 29, 34). Solomon wrote over 3000 proverbs, many of which are collected in the book of Proverbs.

Solomon points us forward to a much greater king—the Lord Jesus—but Jesus is so much more than simply a wise man. In his letter to the Colossians (2:2–3), Paul writes how he longs for them to 'have the full riches of complete understanding, in order that they may know the mystery of God, namely Christ, in whom are hidden all the treasures of wisdom and knowledge'.

As we delve into the opening chapters of Proverbs, I hope that you are propelled towards Jesus. He is the embodiment of true wisdom and he shows us what truly wise living looks like. There was so much I could have said, and I fear I have only scratched the surface. I pray that this time next week, we will have a clearer view of true wisdom and a greater desire to be truly wise women.

The gateway to wisdom

The fear of the Lord is the beginning of knowledge, but fools despise wisdom and instruction.

These opening verses of Proverbs are a like a film trailer: they are meant to whet our appetite for wisdom, to draw us into the book. We live in God's world, but it is a fallen world and we constantly meet situations that are hard or tempting or perplexing. Wisdom is the tool that God gives us to navigate this world. We need discernment, discretion and insight as we search for God's eternal and profound order in this sometimes baffling 21st-century world.

If these verses are like a movie trailer, then the rating for wisdom is Universal. Everyone needs to listen up and attain wisdom—the young, the simple and the wise. No one is beyond the reach of wisdom. It doesn't matter where we are on the IQ spectrum or how old we are in years of age or faith; the path of wisdom is one on which we all need to walk.

How do we embark on this walk of the wise? The key is in verse 7: 'The fear of the Lord is the beginning of knowledge.' We need to come humbly before the awesome God of the whole universe, acknowledging our sin and our need for a Saviour. The first step on the path marked 'wisdom' is to trust Christ, 'in whom are hidden all the treasures of wisdom and knowledge' (Colossians 2:3).

The fear of the Lord is like a gateway into the world of wisdom. The Lord we worship is not a pocket-sized, man-made idol. He is awesome and we need to come to him acknowledging that he is God and we are not. Then we may rejoice that we can walk through that gateway, as women reverently fearing the Lord, and on to the wonderful path of the wise.

Lord, help me to come to you with humility and a desire to grow in wisdom. Help me to be teachable and never to despise your instruction.
                                                                KATY JACK

The source of wisdom

For the Lord gives wisdom; from his mouth come knowledge and understanding.

The fear of the Lord is the gateway through which we walk on to the path of wisdom. As you read today's passage, ponder the urgency with which the father encourages his son to pursue wisdom. This walk to wisdom is no passive Sunday afternoon stroll. It is a deeply purposeful mission, requiring real commitment, with our eyes on the prize—a deeper understanding of the Lord (v. 5).

See how it is that the Lord will keep us walking on the right path: 'The Lord gives wisdom, and from his mouth come knowledge and understanding' (v. 6). Where do I hear God speak? In the pages of my Bible! 2 Timothy 3:16 describes scripture as 'God-breathed', equipping the Christian for every good work—that is, walking the path of the righteous.

I am challenged by this verse. So often, I come to my Bible out of a sense of duty and mentally tick it off as a job done for the day. How different my attitude would be if I truly grasped that, in the power of the Spirit, I can hear God speaking through the words of my Bible. Then I would open my Bible with a sense of great anticipation, wondering what precious gems the Lord might reveal to me today.

That is thrilling in itself, but there's more. Meditate for a couple of minutes on verses 6–11 and contemplate the promises to those walking on this path of wisdom. God's protection is so much more profound and solid than the superficial advice offered by life coaches or magazine articles. God promises that as we immerse ourselves in his word, mining treasures from his lips, his wisdom will enter deep into our hearts and souls.

The challenge for us is to discover how we can be more diligent in seeking God's wisdom.

Help me, Lord, to believe that the Bible is your word and you speak through it. Help me to hunger more for your word and to know the peace and protection of walking the path of wisdom.

KATY JACK

Walking with the wise

Thus you will walk in the ways of the good and keep to the paths of the righteous.

Today we see that there is an alternative to the path of the wise. This path is a dark one; its ways are crooked and devious and it is filled with people who delight in wrongdoing and the perverseness of evil (vv. 13–15). Along this path lives Madam Adulteress, who wants to lure men away to her house. This path leads to death.

There are two paths to choose from and, when we compare them, the choice seems obvious. Of course we want to be on the straight path that leads to life! So why do we sometimes feel so strongly the pull of the wicked? Why does the path of folly sometimes look so attractive? Because the immediate thrill can be blinding. But God doesn't want us to be blind. He wants us to see, to take the long view to the ultimate destination and to stay on the path of the wise.

One of the ways we can make sure this happens is by choosing our walking companions carefully. Verse 20 urges us to walk closely with other Christians. Are you walking with good, godly women? Do you have Christian friends helping you, spurring you on in your walk? My sister is very ill and today, as I write, she is at hospital, finding out if her cancer has spread. It's tempting to ask where God is in this, and to hear the voice of wicked men, louder than the voice of my heavenly Father. But I just received a text from a good, godly friend. It simply said, 'Through the storm, he is Lord, Lord of all.' What a blessing a Christian friend is as we seek to walk the path of the righteous.

Lord, thank you for the blessing and protection of walking with the wise. Help me to cultivate these relationships, and protect me this day from those who would draw me away from the path of righteousness.

KATY JACK

Better than satnav

Trust in the Lord with all your heart and lean not on your own understanding; in all your ways acknowledge him, and he will make your paths straight.

We recently moved to Dorset. In our first few weeks I got to know many 'alternative' routes as I stubbornly refused my husband's offer of sat-nav and insisted that I could drive and read a map at the same time. I capitulated in January and now have a helpful satnav giving me clear, timely instructions on each journey—genius! I trust the satnav and so I acknowledge all that it tells me to do—and I get to my destination with no U-turns.

God is the ultimate satnav for life. Proverbs 3:5–6 urges us to trust in the Lord with all our heart, not because he has a satellite tracking device on us but because he made the heavens and the earth and everything in them (vv. 19–20). His ways are so far beyond us, it is impossible to get our heads around how awesome he is, but if we got just a glimpse each day of his greatness and power and wisdom, how much more we would be able to trust in him with all our heart and not judge things with our own wisdom.

We are urged to acknowledge God in all our ways, to allow him to be Lord of everything (our relationships, our jobs, our homes, our dreams and desires) and to know that under his caring Lordship he will make our path straight—no U-turns. God's wisdom is embroidered on the very fabric of creation; everything operates on the basis of his wisdom. Living in God's world but ignoring his wisdom is like saying, 'I don't believe in gravity' and jumping off a skyscraper: it's foolish and deadly. Allowing God to be *my* God is the surest way to stay on the straight path to life.

Please help me, Lord, in all that I encounter today, to trust in you with all my heart and not to lean on my own understanding. Help me to acknowledge you and your Lordship in everything I do.

KATY JACK

Matters of the heart

Above all else, guard your heart, for it is the wellspring of life.

By this stage you will have got the big idea of Proverbs: wisdom is from God, it is wonderful and we should do all that we can to attain it. Chapter 4 is no exception. Look at the passion with which the father urges his child to get wisdom, and meditate on the benefits that such pursuit will bring.

The contrast between the straight path of wisdom (where steps are unhampered and safe) and the path of the wicked (where evil lurks, waiting to do its worst) is stark. The father is desperate for his child to choose the right path and stay on it, so he provides some very practical tips for the journey. Above all else, he instructs his child to guard his heart (v. 23).

A close relative of mine has heart disease. He takes daily medication, watches his diet and has regular cardiograms and checkups. Heart disease is serious because the heart is essential for physical life, but the 'heart' mentioned in verse 23 is much more than a bodily organ. It refers to our inner being, our soul, the wellspring of life. The state of our spiritual heart is of paramount importance, but when was the last time you had a spiritual cardiogram?

Life is so busy that I find it hard to take time out and examine my heart. Pause now and give yourself a spiritual heart check. Think of unhelpful attitudes that are creeping in, resentments that are growing, or ambitions that are not of God. Perhaps make up your mind not to take a second look at things that harm your heart. Instead, let your eyes look straight ahead on the path of righteousness, with 'the first gleam of dawn shining ever brighter till the full light of day' (v. 18).

Help me, Lord, to guard my heart against anything that would pull me away from you. Please make my heart incline towards you and your ways more and more.

KATY JACK

Flee!

Do not let your heart turn to her ways or stray into her paths... Her house is a highway to the grave, leading down to the chambers of death.

The picture created for us in Proverbs 7 is a sad one. A naïve young man is caught off guard by someone else's wife. She is attractive, prepared and persuasive. She easily leads the young man astray, and we are left in no doubt as to how serious the results of this adulterous seduction will be. He is described as an ox going to the slaughter or a deer stepping into a noose. This exciting clandestine thrill will cost him his life.

What a contrast to our culture's view of adultery! Adultery is everywhere—on the television, in celebrity gossip magazines, at the school gate and, sadly, even in our churches. Society has managed to normalise it. I recently saw a big advert at a bus stop for a website that enables married people to have an affair: how incredibly sad! Society wants to say that adultery is just a normal part of life, so go with your heart, but our passage today shows us that adultery is not normal. We are urged not to let our heart turn towards it, as it is a 'highway to the grave'.

Whatever our marital status, this issue is relevant for us today. If you are married, pray for God's protection on yourself and your husband. If you are single, ask God to protect you from attraction to a married man. Pray for our society, that it would stop listening to the seductive voice of the adulteress. Pray for friends and family living with the tragic outworking of broken relationships all around us. We can all praise God for his promise-keeping, faithful character. Praise him that in his wisdom he designed relationships to be committed and true, just like him.

Please help me, Lord, not to listen to the seductions of adultery but to be captivated by your faithfulness always.

KATY JACK

Invitations of wisdom and folly

The fear of the Lord is the beginning of wisdom, and knowledge of the Holy One is understanding.

As we finish our week in Proverbs, we close with Lady Wisdom and Madam Folly setting out their stalls, showing their wares, seeking to attract customers. See how different they are!

Lady Wisdom has built her own strong house. She has prepared her own food, mixed her own wine and set her table. She longs to cast the net of her invitation to wisdom as wide as possible, so she calls from the highest point in the city and sends out her maids. Her invitation is clear: 'Come, leave your former life, eat of my supplies, and follow me. You will walk in the way of understanding and you will live' (see vv. 5–6).

Contrast this with the offer made by Madam Folly. She is undisciplined and without knowledge but that doesn't stop her trying to shout loudly over the voice of wisdom at the high point of the city. Her opening gambit is the same: 'Let all who are simple come in here' (v. 16), but her stolen water and food are to be consumed in secret. That is where her advert stops: she can't offer long life or the way of understanding. She doesn't mention that those who have taken up her offer are dead: her previous guests are in the depths of the grave.

The parallels with the Lord Jesus and Satan are striking. Satan can make things look and sound so attractive, so enticing and tempting, but the Lord Jesus is the one on whom we need to build our lives. If you have time, read Luke 6:46–49. Are you building wisely or foolishly? How can you listen to Jesus more? He is supremely worthy of our devotion and attention. As Peter said, where else can we go, when Jesus alone has the words of eternal life? (John 6:68).

Lord, please help me to be a wise woman. Help me to listen to you and your words and to build my life on you.

KATY JACK

Making links

Claire Musters writes:

I have been a worship leader for many years now, which means I think about the subject of worship quite regularly and extensively. I've also read a lot of books about it. That by no means makes me an expert, as we will spend our whole lives learning more about worshipping our king. However, the thing that stands out for me when I read about worship leading is that it is not my responsibility to ensure people are worshipping on a Sunday: it should come naturally to them, out of an overflow of a constantly worshipping heart.

Worship is our heart's response to the God we serve and love, yet so often it is simply constrained to the songs we sing and the role we have on a Sunday morning. We can worship God just as much in the craziness of the Monday morning rush hour or school run, or when doing the cleaning or washing, as we can in a corporate 'time of worship'. God longs to be involved in all the little details of our daily lives and is passionate about spending time with us, whatever we are doing. This is not to belittle worship: it is costly and demanding, and we'll be looking at that aspect of it, too. While God wants us to learn to connect with him constantly, throughout our day, he also wishes us to hide away with him at regular intervals. It is in those quieter times that we are refreshed and can hear his voice more clearly.

There is much in scripture to teach us about worship and much that can surprise and challenge us. For instance, there is plenty about obedience and sacrifice flowing from a thankful heart. I hope we can approach these next few weeks with an openness and willingness to be challenged and changed. We'll begin by asking God to speak to us afresh about cultivating a much deeper lifestyle of worship. Let's go on a journey of discovery together!

Wired for worship

For in him all things were created: things in heaven and on earth, visible and invisible, whether thrones or powers or rulers or authorities; all things have been created through him and for him.

I think it is important to start by dwelling on the fact that everyone on this earth was made for worship; it is built into us. We were made by God, for God. If we are not worshipping God, we are worshipping something else.

'Worship' comes from an Old English word meaning 'worthiness', and it really is about honouring what we value the most. As Louie Giglio says, in his book *The Air I Breathe: Worship as a way of life* (Multnomah, 2006), 'Right this very instant, all across your city or town, people of all shapes and sizes, people of every age and purpose are doing it—continually making decisions based on what they value most. Worship happens everywhere… all day long.' When we look at it from this perspective, the idea of 'worship as a lifestyle' doesn't seem so alien.

Today's Bible passage tells us that Jesus existed before time, helped his Father to create the world and has also reconciled us to God. As verse 17 indicates, 'He existed before anything else, and he holds all creation together' (NLT). There is so much in this passage to think about: try reading through it slowly again and see how your spirit responds to the enormous truths contained in it.

You may not feel like worshipping God today. Life is hard and none of us is immune to difficult circumstances. Even if you don't feel it, though, the way you live your life reveals what it is that you worship. Your ideals and priorities are all based on what you value most. That is simply the way you were made. If you, like me, have a tendency towards self-sufficiency, you might find it really helpful to ponder the question below.

Think about what you prioritise in terms of your time and money. What does it reveal to you about the things you value most?

CLAIRE MUSTERS

God reveals; we respond

The heavens declare the glory of God; the skies proclaim the work of his hands. Day after day they pour forth speech; night after night they reveal knowledge.

Looking back through the books I have read on worship, I was struck once more by how many of them focused on worship as a response to what we know about God. This makes a lot of sense, as it is only out of revelation that we can make a heartfelt response, and yet how often do we try to worship out of a dry and unfed bank of revelation? One writer suggests that if we are not very good at worshipping, it's simply because we don't know our God very well. Ouch! I know there are times in life when worshipping is harder, and we will look at that issue specifically later on, but there is a basic truth in this writer's view.

So where should we go to find out more about God? His word is the obvious place, and a great starting point is the Psalms, such as the one we've read today. It's there that we learn of the awesomeness of God and are reminded that he knows even the number of hairs on our heads and wants a personal relationship with us. What incredible truths!

Spend some time absorbing these verses. The more science discovers about the universe, the more we can be in awe of the God who created it all. It's mind-blowing to consider that such an awesome God also knows every intimate detail of our lives and wants to spend time with us.

I love the way that Psalm 19 paints such a vivid picture of God's own creation literally pulsating with the truth about him—that everything reveals his glory. It also reveals how God's laws and commands are ordered and right. That, to me, shows his care for humanity.

Sit quietly and write down some of the things this psalm reveals to you about God. Try to write a response in the form of a prayer, thank you letter, psalm or song.

CLAIRE MUSTERS

In the Spirit and in truth

'Yet a time is coming and has now come when the true worshippers will worship the Father in the Spirit and in truth, for they are the kind of worshippers the Father seeks.'

In this passage, Jesus teaches us about the importance of attitude rather than place of worship. Here the Samaritan woman is bowled over by how much this man knows about her and recognises that he must be a prophet. So she changes the subject and asks him a popular theological question of the day: where is the correct place to worship? 'Our ancestors worshipped on this mountain, but you Jews claim that the place where we must worship is in Jerusalem' (v. 20).

Jesus' answer is one of the most important teachings on worship that he ever gave: 'Believe me, a time is coming when you will worship the Father neither on this mountain nor in Jerusalem… God is spirit, and his worshippers must worship in the Spirit and in truth' (vv. 21, 24). In this statement, Jesus was revealing the importance of attitude rather than location when we worship. He also spoke of the importance of the Spirit as well as truth, as it is through the Spirit that we are able to connect with God and celebrate the truths that we know about him. The Bible clearly teaches that we are all born of the Spirit when we become Christians (Ephesians 1:13–14), which means that we can each draw on his wisdom and strength day by day.

Sadly, sometimes our Westernised worship culture can become a smokescreen if we get too caught up in it, hiding us from God rather than drawing us near. The means by which we worship should always remain that—the means, not the end. It is not about the latest songs or the 'best' worship leader. Although I enjoy singing new songs, putting too much emphasis on them is merely a distraction from true worship.

Do you have a tendency to focus on the songs and musical arrangements rather than God when you take part in corporate worship? Ask God to help you to focus on him alone.

CLAIRE MUSTERS

Lips that praise/lips that curse

'What goes into someone's mouth does not defile them, but what comes out of their mouth, that is what defiles them.'

Here Jesus is challenging the Pharisees and teachers of the law who are trying to trip him up. He closely reflects what is said in Isaiah 29:13: 'These people come near to me with their mouth and honour me with their lips, but their hearts are far from me. Their worship of me is based on merely human rules they have been taught.'

Jesus is trying to make them understand that worship is not about paying lip service. He explains that it is what comes out of a person's mouth that makes them unclean, because (as he says in Luke 6:45) 'the mouth speaks what the heart is full of'. This is a sobering thought and prompts me to ask: what are you like when no one is looking? In church or at work, we can put on a show of behaving like Christians, but behind closed doors the reality can be very different. The one whom we profess to follow and worship sees it all and knows us to the very depths of our beings. What he wants from us is a walk of worship that is full of integrity, day in day out.

'Out of the same mouth come praise and cursing. My brothers and sisters, this should not be,' says James 3:10. This verse reveals to me that part of our daily worship is to keep a check on our tongues, and I know that this is an area I need to work on further. Words of healing and words that cut and hurt can come out of the very same mouth at various times in a day, but James reminds us that, if this is happening, there is something very wrong going on.

'May these words of my mouth and this meditation of my heart be pleasing in your sight, Lord, my Rock and my Redeemer' (Psalm 19:14).
CLAIRE MUSTERS

Jesus' sacrifice

Through Jesus, therefore, let us continually offer to God a sacrifice of praise—the fruit of lips that openly profess his name.

I believe that this passage is a great reminder of our need for a Saviour and of the ultimate sacrifice he had to make. Before Jesus came, communion with God was possible only through a hugely complicated set of rules and animal sacrifices. Jesus' death did away with such rituals and opened up the way to the Father.

Let's ponder Jesus' sacrifice a little more. Remember the agonising struggle that he had in Gethsemane when he thought about what was going to happen to him? Take a look at Matthew 26:36–46. 'My soul is overwhelmed' seems like a very apt description, but somewhat inadequate, too! In his humanity, he must have been petrified at this point, but he was still able to pray, 'Yet not as I will, but as you will.' Thank goodness he was able to do that, as it is only through what he suffered and endured on the cross, and conquered through his resurrection, that we are able to have a relationship with God. Today we are able to worship God freely, without needing a priest as a go-between.

Although Jesus paid the price for our sins in a way that we are totally incapable of doing for ourselves, God does still ask us for sacrifice. We are told to take up our cross on a daily basis (Luke 9:23). We are also asked to put others before ourselves (Philippians 2:1–4). But when we do these things from an attitude of thankfulness and in remembrance of what Jesus has done for us, they don't seem so much of a sacrifice, do they?

Thank you, Lord, for paying the price that I could not pay for my salvation. Help me to live in the light of what you've done, remembering to take up my own personal cross daily.

CLAIRE MUSTERS

Obedience and faith

'Now I know that you fear God, because you have not withheld from me your son, your only son.'

Imagine, for a moment, what is going on between the lines here. At the start of this passage, we are told that God asks Abraham to take his son and sacrifice him on an altar. In the very next verse we are told that Abraham set off the following morning, early, to do just that.

I am curious about what must have been going through Abraham's mind during the night. What an incredible act of obedience, to get up and prepare to do what God has told him to do! He doesn't know that God is going to step in and provide a different object for the offering— even if he does say in faith, when Isaac asks him where the lamb is, that God will provide. (Oh, how deeply Isaac's question must have cut him.) And how must Isaac have felt when Abraham then bound him to the altar? He must have thought his father had gone crazy. Yet then he sees how God steps in, and listens as God makes a promise about Abraham's descendants.

Of course, this episode also gives us a beautiful picture of the way God would, in the future, give up his own Son to death. He stepped in and saved Isaac from the altar, but he had to allow his own Son to suffer in order to save humankind.

We may never be asked to pay such a high price as Abraham or be tested as much as he was, but, when we hear God's clear direction, our act of worship is to be obedient, whatever the cost. Interestingly, in 2 Samuel 24:24, David says, 'I will not sacrifice to the Lord my God burnt offerings that cost me nothing'. In a way, worship needs to cost something—as it then reveals how much God means to us.

When was the last time you offered God something that cost you greatly in terms of personal sacrifice?

CLAIRE MUSTERS

Worship is service

Take your everyday, ordinary life—your sleeping, eating, going-to-work, and walking-around life—and place it before God as an offering.

This passage focuses on the fact that our everyday lives should be about keeping in step with God. THE MESSAGE is great at putting this point across. I like the challenge it gives us right at the start not to be moulded by our culture, as we can all slip into that danger so easily, without realising it.

The richness of truth in today's reading is amazing, but much of it is very simple and matter-of-fact: if we focus on God, simply doing what he asks us to do, he will change us for the better. We should find out what God wants us to work at, then focus on doing just that. The image of the body used in verses 4–6 is a vivid picture of how each of us has a God-ordained function.

Worship is not just about what we say but also about what we do. Colossians 3:23–24 sums up how we can worship through daily tasks: 'Whatever you do, work at it with all your heart, as working for the Lord, not for human masters, since… it is the Lord Christ you are serving.'

The second part of our passage today covers so much of what we can do within a life of worship (loving each other, helping those in need, living at peace and looking after ourselves so that we don't burn out). Each one of these elements is an important aspect of worship. 1 John 3:17–18 goes so far as to say, 'If anyone has material possessions and sees a brother or sister in need but has no pity on them, how can the love of God be in that person? Dear children, let us not love with words or speech but with actions and in truth.' Sobering stuff…

Have you ever considered helping the poor, or fulfilling your role within the church family, to be an act of worship? How should this idea change your attitude towards such things?

CLAIRE MUSTERS

Find time to withdraw

'Lord, don't you care that my sister has left me to do the work by myself?'... 'Mary has chosen what is better, and it will not be taken away from her.'

Here, Jesus is tackling our natural tendency to busy ourselves doing 'stuff'. Honestly, I find it hard to stop (even to spend time with God) before I've done all the jobs that need doing, and yet, when I put time with God first, my perspective on those jobs changes. When I ask for his help with the tasks on my 'to do' list that really do still need doing, often I find a renewed energy and focus. Things that I thought would take me a long time are done much more quickly.

Jesus is also making a very pertinent comment about our acts of service. I said in yesterday's comment that worship is service, and that is true, but the heart behind it is the crux of the matter. I have deliberately put these two readings next to each other because I think we can often busy ourselves with commendable tasks but neglect the love relationship that is meant to be behind them, fuelling them. Feeding and caring for the guests were necessary jobs (and I'm on Martha's side to a large extent here!) and yet we can go overboard and miss out on the very thing that we truly desire and need—time with, and input from, our Lord. How often do we overcomplicate things that could be done in a simpler way, which would free us up to spend time with him? How often, too, do we run out of energy doing things that God hasn't called us to do? We need to take time to sit at his feet as Mary did, drawing from the source so that we can serve others out of the overflow he has given us, not from our own limited strength.

How often do you rush about trying to achieve things, while neglecting time spent at your Saviour's feet? Repent and spend some quality time with him today.

CLAIRE MUSTERS

Are you ever 'undignified'?

Wearing a linen ephod, David was dancing before the Lord with all his might... [David said] 'I will become even more undignified than this.'

Now, be honest in your response to the question I'm about to ask you. Who did you relate to most when you read today's passage? The carefree king, totally immersed in worshipping his God, or his wife, embarrassed by his 'show', who felt that his behaviour should have been more suited to his royal status? To put it in a modern-day context, how often have you looked at the slightly strange dancers in church, the flag wavers or the 'groaners', and wished they weren't in your congregation? Have you ever been upset by something your church leader has suggested, or allowed, because it didn't seem 'respectful' enough for church?

I want to challenge us all to consider if we are too busy thinking about other people's view of us to worship freely—and f we are imposing our notions of what worship should look like on to others. David wasn't worried about anyone around him because he was concentrating on an audience of one—his Lord. Even when Michal challenged him over his actions, he said that he would be even more undignified, given the chance. What a great retort!

When was the last time you felt abandoned in worship? If it is out of the overflow of our hearts that we worship, doesn't it follow that sometimes we should be a little 'crazy', doing something out of our normal comfort zones? I know that most people reading this will be British, like myself, and I also know that I'm quite a reserved person and I enjoy the fact that I'm usually standing behind my keyboard during corporate times of worship, but these are side issues. God wants our hearts to be so captivated by his truths, which transcend our nationality and personality, that we can't help but worship him fully.

I am sorry, Lord, that I allow my insecurity about other people's opinions of me to hold me back. Help me to learn how to be abandoned to you in worship.

CLAIRE MUSTERS

Sing your song!

'I will sing to the Lord, for he is highly exalted. Both horse and driver he has hurled into the sea. The Lord is my strength and my defence; he has become my salvation. He is my God, and I will praise him, my father's God, and I will exalt him.'

Here, Moses and the Israelite people sing a song of great victory, giving glory to God for the miraculous crossing of the Red Sea. At the end of the passage, we are told that Miriam took up her tambourine and led all the women into their own song and dance.

I want to encourage you today to recognise that we all have a song to sing. Psalm 40:3 says, 'He put a new song in my mouth, a hymn of praise to our God', so let your song bubble up and sing it out. Too often we can allow ourselves to be silenced, but Miriam didn't—and we should be like her.

There will be specific songs for specific times: look at this passage to see how the Israelites' song responded directly to what God had just done for them. When was the last time you sang out a song of thanks to God for an answer to prayer? Whether you have a good voice or not is not the issue. The Bible describes incense as 'sweet smoke' and it is used as an image for our prayers, worship and praise. Indeed, 2 Corinthians 2:15 says that 'we are to God the pleasing aroma of Christ'. Just as Christ's death on the cross washes us clean of our sins and allows us to come close to our heavenly Father, so, I believe, it turns any out-of-tune, ear-piercing songs into a delightful sound. If you're not too sure you agree with me, think about a child doing something for the first time. It's not important whether they have perfected the skill or not: their parents still well up with pride to see them try. God is longing to hear your voice today, so won't you sing to him with the words he has already placed on your heart?

Spend some time thinking back over what God has done for you in recent months, then let your thankfulness bubble out of you as a song.

CLAIRE MUSTERS

Worshipping through suffering

After they had been severely flogged, they were thrown into prison, and the jailer was commanded to guard them carefully... About midnight Paul and Silas were praying and singing hymns to God.

One of the Christian women I admire most is my mum. She suffers from lupus and also has rheumatoid arthritis. She finds it hard to breathe and is in constant pain, but nothing makes her faith waver: it may dwindle to a tiny flicker at times but it is always there. I find that incredible. So I don't write about this subject lightly.

Imagine how much Paul and Silas must have been suffering, yet they chose to praise God despite their circumstances. The result: they were set loose from their chains and they showed their integrity to the jailer by not running away. They then led his whole family to the Lord. I'm not saying there will always be such a positive outcome to everyone's pain—just that there could be. My mum has been to hospital countless times and is usually desperate not to go in, yet often she testifies to some 'God-incidence' in which she was able to talk to someone who was dying or suffering badly. Each time, she is able to say that if she was admitted simply to speak to that person, the pain was worth it.

I wish I could lift my head above my circumstances like that more often. This is the crux of the matter: it's a choice we make. When we look at our circumstances and the physical reality, we can either allow ourselves to slide downwards or we can acknowledge the suffering but also choose to remember that God's sovereignty doesn't change in the light of it.

God knows how you are feeling, so be honest—but don't stay in the doldrums. The Psalms are made up of 70 per cent laments; take a look at some and note how, even in the depths of despair, the writers lift their eyes heavenward, speaking out truths about God's greatness. For our own sake, we need to learn to do the same.

Use what Habakkuk said, even in the light of impending starvation and devastation, as a starting point for your own prayer: 'Yet I will rejoice in the Lord, I will be joyful in God my Saviour' (Habakkuk 3:18).

CLAIRE MUSTERS

Make space for the extravagant

A woman in that town who lived a sinful life… came there with an alabaster jar of perfume. As she stood behind him at his feet weeping, she began to wet his feet with her tears. Then she wiped them with her hair, kissed them and poured perfume on them.

What total extravagance! Could you picture yourself entering a home uninvited, weeping, wiping Jesus' feet with your hair and then kissing them and pouring perfume worth a year's salary over them? Jesus not only accepted the offering of worship from this woman but also told her that her faith had saved her. Others looked on, probably shocked that Jesus allowed such a 'sinner' near him and appalled at the apparent waste of money (which is the way the disciples responded to a similar incident later in Jesus' ministry: see Matthew 26:6–13).

Before we side with the onlookers, condemning the sinner as inappropriate and her actions as too 'showy' (do we condemn people in the same way at church?), think about how she truly understood the depth of her sin. She wept enough tears to clean Jesus' feet. She knew who she was and her dire need of Jesus, and, as she poured out her love extravagantly, he forgave her extravagantly, extending his love and forgiveness to her.

Extravagant means 'excessive', 'lavish' and 'wasteful'. Worship that can be described in this way is our natural response when we truly understand what we've been saved from. I am enjoying a song by Kim Walker Smith at the moment, which includes the line, 'I wanna waste myself on you'. The words seemed strange at first, but they have been hitting my heart each time I listen to the song, and, looking at this passage, I can see exactly what they mean. Just as in any other love relationship, God enjoys it when we show him how much we love him. This woman poured out something so precious that others called her wasteful, yet Jesus understood her extravagant act and praised her for it. Could he do the same to you?

What extravagant act can you do today to show God how much you love him?

CLAIRE MUSTERS

Sometimes worship is a battle

Jesus said to him, 'Away from me, Satan! For it is written: "Worship the Lord your God, and serve him only."'

Matthew tells us that Jesus had just fasted for 40 days and 40 nights, and he was hungry (v. 2). What an understatement! Then Satan came to tempt him with something to ease his discomfort. If Satan used this method with Jesus, he will certainly try it with us. Sometimes our everyday worship is simply about standing strong against our enemy, refusing to give in to temptation.

See how Satan even used scripture to try to catch Jesus out, but Jesus was able to quote portions back at him. It is important that we know our Bibles well enough not to be swayed by false teaching or other lies from our enemy. We also need to make sure we are equipped for battle. Not long ago, I was challenged about the fact that I spend time each morning choosing what to wear, but often forget about 'dressing' my spirit. I now try to consciously 'put on' the fruit of the Spirit in Galatians 5:22–23 (love, joy, peace, and so on). I also realised that I had stopped putting on the 'armour of God', so I try to make it part of my daily morning worship by reading through Ephesians 6:13–17 and visualising putting on the armour.

We are also called to join with our fellow believers as a united army. As a worship leader, I am intrigued by the fact that it was the musicians who led the Israelite army in procession. 2 Chronicles 20:21 tells us, 'Jehoshaphat appointed men to sing to the Lord and to praise him for the splendour of his holiness as they went out at the head of the army, saying: "Give thanks to the Lord, for his love endures for ever."' Worship can truly be our battle cry and is an important way to fuel our faith during seasons of attack.

Read Ephesians 6:10–18 and imagine putting on each part of the armour so that you are equipped for the day.

CLAIRE MUSTERS

Worship and justice

'Away with the noise of your songs! I will not listen to the music of your harps. But let justice roll on like a river, righteousness like a never-failing stream!'

It was with great interest, and an ever-softening heart, that I read *The Art of Compassion*. Martin Smith, formerly of the band Delirious?, had launched the charity CompassionArt and invited other musicians to write an album with him, the proceeds of which went to helping the poor. I cried buckets reading the book, in which each artist revealed why they had come to be involved. For many, being part of today's Western-ised worship music culture had made them desperate to discover the true meaning of worship afresh. One by one they shared how God had led them to Amos 5:23–24 and how deeply they had been touched by these verses. God doesn't want our empty words: he doesn't want us to sing about how much we love him on a Sunday, then turn away from a person in desperate need on Monday morning.

Many of the artists involved in the charity have taken their families out to Africa to visit orphanages and have also adopted children and brought them home. I realise that most of us don't have the money to take our children abroad to make them more aware of worldwide needs, but God does hold us accountable for caring for the people we meet daily.

When the Israelites were complaining that they were religiously fast-ing but God hadn't noticed, God replied, 'Is not this the kind of fasting I have chosen: to loose the chains of injustice and untie the cords of the yoke, to set the oppressed free and break every yoke?' (Isaiah 58:6). In Matthew 25:45 Jesus says, 'Whatever you did not do for one of the least of these, you did not do for me.'

We may not feel that we have much to offer, but when we reach out to those around us, God ministers to them. Being his hands and feet in this world is a vital part of worship.

If you are not sure where the most needy people are, start praying that God will open your eyes to see who he wants you to help and how you can bring his justice to your neighbourhood.

CLAIRE MUSTERS

Making links

Alie Teale writes:

'Righteousness exalts a nation, but sin condemns any people' (Proverbs 14:34, NIV).

Over the next two weeks we are going to be looking at some themes from the book of Amos. I can't remember ever reading Amos from beginning to end. I do remember the visions of the basket of fruit and the plumbline, from the few Scripture lessons on the minor prophets that we had when I was at school, but that was a very long time ago. So, if your experience is anything like mine, I hope we are going to discover some new things in the word of God together.

The name 'Amos' means 'burden bearer'. Amos carried the heavy burden of responsibility for bringing God's message of judgement on Israel around the year 760BC, just before a catastrophic earthquake shook that area of the Middle East, and about four decades before the Assyrians invaded and completely defeated Israel.

Amos came from a rural background: he was a shepherd and also tended an orchard of sycamore figs in Tekoa, a small town about 15 miles south of Jerusalem. He would have been shaped by the context in which he had grown up, so life in Jerusalem and the bustle and corruption of city life would have stood in stark contrast to his early experience. When conditions deteriorate in a society, community or organisation, it is usually necessary for someone to come in from the outside with a different perspective, to put their finger on what has gone wrong. Then the situation can be rectified and a new course set for the future.

Amos's head must have been in a whirl. He spoke out against the social, political, economic, military and religious conditions of the time, addressing not only Israel but also the surrounding nations. Self-service and materialism were never intended as God's foundation for abundant living: God's covenant declared that he would bless the people of Israel so that they could be a blessing to others, not so that they could keep the blessing for themselves. We can learn from their experience that our lives are meant to be a blessing to others.

Enough is enough

The Lord has spoken... 'You only have I chosen of all the families of the earth; therefore I will punish you for all your sins.'... When a trumpet sounds in a city, do not the people tremble?

When God called Abraham to leave his home and travel to a place God would show him, God said to Abraham, 'I will make you into a great nation, and I will bless you; I will make your name great, and you will be a blessing. I will bless those who bless you, and whoever curses you I will curse; and all peoples on earth will be blessed through you' (Genesis 12:2–3).

This is what we call the Abrahamic covenant, and the first part of this covenant contains a wonderful promise. Being very much focused on the individual and our own needs, we tend to forget, or even ignore, the fact that with this promise of blessing came great responsibility. Abraham and his descendants were not to keep the blessing for themselves, but were expected to share it so that all the nations would be blessed through them.

We might ask what this blessing might be. Put very simply, God's blessing is for every individual to be in a right relationship with him, to enjoy his presence and to be able to worship him in righteousness and truth. In the time of Amos, the people of Israel had forgotten the responsibility that came with the promise. They were focused on themselves and their own needs—so much so that they had become a bad example to the nations around them. God tells them through Amos that enough is enough: they need to be different from other nations and be a witness to the Lord of heaven and earth (compare Deuteronomy 28:9–10).

Through the new covenant in Christ, we share in the same blessing. Are we shirking our responsibilities? Is there anything in our lives to which God is saying, 'Enough is enough'?

Lord, forgive me for the compromises in my life—the glaring ones and the subtle ones. Put your finger on those that offend you and help me change my ways.

ALIE TEALE

Measured and found wanting

This is what the Lord says: 'For three sins of Judah, even for four, I will not relent. Because they have rejected the law of the Lord and have not kept his decrees, because they have been led astray by false gods, the gods their ancestors followed, I will send fire on Judah.'

Perhaps you struggle with the type of Old Testament prophecy that Walter Brueggeman calls 'announcements of judgement', the kind that calls down God's wrath on transgressors. We much prefer 'announcements of salvation', which promise us God's immeasurable blessing and a bright, happy future. What we forget (or perhaps do not even realise) is that God has no desire for these announcements of judgement to be fulfilled. His prophets bring these stern words to the people to wake them up to the situation in and around them. Rather like fish swimming in dirty water, they have become so used to the murk and filth that they think it is normal. Only a voice from the outside has the objectivity and clarity to shine God's light into such situations, to wake people out of their stupor so that they have the chance to see the truth of their position and make a change.

In today's passage, the prophet is rubbing the message in hard. The repetition of the phrase 'for three sins… even for four, I will not relent' is a device used to emphasise that the Lord has 'measured' the people's sin and rebellion. He is distressed by their return to the pagan gods that their ancestors followed before he revealed himself to them as the one true God, Creator of heaven and earth. Can you hear God's pleading in these words, rather than his ire? Nevertheless, God is a holy God and, if repentance is not forthcoming, he will not relent. Israel was eventually invaded and destroyed.

How long will the Lord tolerate our acts of rebellion? If you hear his voice ringing in your ears, do not harden your heart; he is waiting for you with open arms.

'Test me, Lord, and try me, examine my heart and my mind; for I have always been mindful of your unfailing love and have lived in reliance on your faithfulness' (Psalm 26:2–3).

ALIE TEALE

The weight of judgement

'Now then, I will crush you as a cart crushes when loaded with grain. The swift will not escape, the strong will not muster their strength, and the warrior will not save his life… Even the bravest warriors will flee naked on that day,' declares the Lord.

Recently I worked at a part-time job on a Sunday afternoon. I'd managed to negotiate my hours so that I could get to church and I was excited about the prospect of the necessary extra income. On the second weekend, some of us were chatting about workplace attitudes while we waited for the delivery van to return. I partially shared an experience from a job I had 30 years ago, to illustrate how attitudes to women had changed in the workplace over three decades. My colleagues pushed me for more details and eventually I gave in, divulging some inappropriate words that had been said to me. As soon as the words were out of my mouth, I regretted saying them. One member of the group expressed how offended they felt by what I had said, since they had just come from church.

What I had shared was not my opinion, but a report of what had been said to me by several other colleagues during my second job in my early 20s. Even so, I felt totally crushed. I felt as if I had let the side down, especially as I had just come from church, too. Feeling as I did, the rest of the afternoon did not go well and I was glad to get home when it was over. Thankfully, in the quiet of my kitchen I was able to remember that we don't need to be crushed by our failings because Jesus was 'crushed for our iniquities; the punishment that brought us peace was on him, and by his wounds we are healed' (Isaiah 53:5).

When you feel the crushing weight of your own lack of judgement or blatant wrongdoing, come to Jesus. Your suffering can be alleviated by him.

'I am feeble and utterly crushed; I groan in anguish of heart. All my longings lie open before you, Lord; my sighing is not hidden from you' (Psalm 38:8–9).

ALIE TEALE

The sound of thunder

He said: 'The Lord roars from Zion and thunders from Jerusalem; the pastures of the shepherds dry up, and the top of Carmel withers.'

When I was a child I lived in Africa. Some nights I would lie awake under my mosquito net and, above the hum of the cicadas, I could often hear lions roaring in the darkness. At other times, when the rain clouds piled up, the thunder rumbled over the escarpment at a volume I never hear in England, before the rain lashed down on the tin roof of our house.

The lion's roar and the rolling thunder are terrifying sounds; both give warning that there are forces of nature at work that threaten our imagined sense of security. Amos used the metaphors of the lion's roar and rolling thunder to symbolise God's impending intervention into the spiritual apathy that characterised the life of Israel and the surrounding nations. The lion's roar is God's protest that social and political conditions have degenerated further than he will tolerate: he is ready to lash out at the perpetrators. The sound of thunder is a picture of God's mounting anger, which will eventually unleash a storm on the people on the earth below.

We see from the verse quoted above that, in Amos's prophecy, God's intervention in the affairs of humankind would result in a severe drought. Carmel was one of the most fertile places in Israel, as well as being the seat of Baal worship, and God would obliterate it. In today's world, many of us have become distanced from the effects of nature on our everyday lives: we have light at the flick of a switch, heat at the turn of a dial, food when there is drought, and shelter that can withstand all but the most violent natural disasters. We have lost touch with the sense that God uses nature to communicate his greatness and his holiness to those he created.

'The Lord will roar from Zion and thunder from Jerusalem… But the Lord will be a refuge for his people, a stronghold for the people of Israel' (Joel 3:16).

ALIE TEALE

Woe to the complacent

Woe to you who are complacent in Zion, and to you who feel secure on Mount Samaria, you notable men of the foremost nation, to whom the people of Israel come!... You will be among the first to go into exile; your feasting and lounging will end.

In Proverbs 14:34 we read, 'Righteousness exalts a nation, but sin condemns any people.' Amos prophesied to a nation trapped in a downward spiral of moral decay, led in that direction by leaders who imagined it was the chief among nations. The truth, though, was far removed from their perceptions: in reality, they were complacent, conceited and full of pride.

Today's passage from Amos is an interesting snapshot of his times and leads us to believe that the leaders of Israel delayed addressing issues that demanded confrontation and diverted their attention with feasting and entertainment rather than getting stuck into the dirty work. How easy it would be to point the same accusation at political and secular leaders today, yet I have increasingly become concerned that the way we run our churches is a reflection of society around us. I mingled with church leaders across a multitude of denominations for three decades and have to admit I always struggled with the degree of entertaining that seemed to have to be done in order to oil the social wheels in a church context. For a while it was flattering to be wined and dined. In turn, I loved cooking 'executive dinners' and 'leaders' lunches'—and the praise I received for the results bolstered the self-confidence I lacked at the time. But the amount that was consumed, and the reckoning of the receipts once the clearing up was done, often left me quietly questioning the necessity of it all in terms of advancing God's kingdom.

My life today is in stark contrast to those times, and it is usually only by contrasts that we are able to assess the true reality of a situation. Are you able to stand outside your own situation and ask the Lord what he deems unnecessary?

Lord, forgive us for our complacency, conceit and pride. We have come from dust and will return to dust. Help us put ourselves and our social lives into your perspective.

ALIE TEALE

FRIDAY 6 FEBRUARY   AMOS 9:1–10 (NIV)

No place to hide

[The Lord said] 'Though they dig down to the depths below, from there my hand will take them. Though they climb up to the heavens above, from there I will bring them down… Though they hide from my eyes at the bottom of the sea, there I will command the serpent to bite them.'

I don't know how well you know the Psalms, but I had a sense of recognition when I read this part of Amos. Have a look at Psalm 139 and read verses 7–12. Can you see the similarity? The construction of the two texts is almost the same: in each case the author presents opposite extremes and gives a poetic description of the impossibility of escaping from God. There is no height, no depth and no distance we can travel to escape him.

We are probably more familiar with Psalm 139, in which the psalmist revels in the fact that we can never be lost to God's presence and that, wherever we go, God's Spirit will be with us, his hand will guide us, his right hand will hold us fast and the dark will become light around us. That knowledge has been a comfort to me and many thousands of Christians down the years, all over the world. Amos, however, turns the sentiments in Psalm 139 on their head: he makes it clear that there is nowhere the Israelites can go to hide from God's wrath.

In the same way, there is nowhere we can hide when we fall short of God's best for us. Recently one of my little dogs made a wet patch on my bed. I was very cross with her and she hid under the bed and wouldn't come out, but I knew where she was and eventually managed to coax her out to kiss and make up. There's no point hiding under the metaphorical bed when we have messed up; let God draw you out of your hiding place and gather you in his arms so that you can put things right.

Lord, when I mess up and want to hide away from you, help me to allow you to draw me out of my hiding place and be reconciled with you.

ALIE TEALE

A basket of fruit

Hear this, you who trample the needy and do away with the poor of the land, saying, 'When will the New Moon be over that we may sell grain, and the Sabbath be ended that we may market wheat?'

The Lord gave Amos a vision of a basket of fruit and said, 'The time is ripe for my people Israel; I will spare them no longer' (v. 2). The reason for this judgement was their desire to hasten the sabbath so that trading could recommence. Then, when trading did recommence, it was unjust: merchants literally took the shoes from people's feet (v. 6).

The basket of fruit in the vision wasn't the usual Western hamper of apples, oranges and pears; the basket was full of sycamore figs. Amos tended a grove of such trees and was very familiar with them (7:14). Part of his job would have included the ancient practice of gashing the unripe fruit to hasten ripening. We know that piercing the fruit in this way produces ethylene, which promotes ripening, but to Amos the image of gashing the fruit in readiness for harvest would have been a violent and injurious one.

The mythology surrounding the sycamore fig would also not have been lost on Amos. Besides being the Egyptian 'tree of life' whose leaves shrouded the boundary between life and death and whose wood was used for funeral caskets, it was also probably the Hebrew 'tree of life' in the garden of Eden. (Why else would Adam and Eve have used fig leaves to cover themselves?) For Amos, this simple basket of fruit was laden with symbolism. Maybe a more immediate image for us would be harvesting apples to be thrown in a cider press and crushed to pulp.

Whatever the fruity metaphor, however, the message is clear: the Lord does not tolerate those with bad business ethics. We all have customers—people we interact with on a daily basis—even if physical goods are not exchanged. How's your customer service? Do you go the extra mile or try to pass off overpriced shoddy goods?

'Blessed are those who act justly, who always do what is right. Remember me, Lord, when you show favour to your people, come to my aid when you save them' (Psalm 106:3–4).

ALIE TEALE

How much is it going to take?

'Many times I struck your gardens and vineyards, destroying them with blight and mildew. Locusts devoured your fig and olive trees, yet you have not returned to me,' declares the Lord.

Today's passage is a litany of complaints from the Lord. He lists all the ways he tried to get the attention of his people in the time of the prophet Amos. He sent a bread famine (maybe the grain silos ran out or spoiled); drought at the height of the growing season, which dried up wells and cisterns; swarms of locusts that devoured valuable cash crops; fungal diseases that destroyed vegetables and fruit; an infection that decimated the human population; war and unrest that incurred human and animal casualties and caused many people to live as refugees in unsanitary conditions.

In my personal experience, it has been the tragic situations in my life that have turned me back to the Lord or thrown me more fully on his grace than in my day-to-day life of faith. I don't believe that the Lord sends pain and suffering to punish us or persuade us to return to him—not in the way that we see described in the Old Testament—but, in the words of C.S. Lewis, I do think that 'suffering is God's megaphone to rouse a deaf world' and it is at times like these that we do turn to him. Personally I have never been so attentive to what God had to say to me through his word and through others than when my brother died in a car wreck in 1985, or in the months after the man to whom I'd committed almost 30 years of my life left his job and his family without any hint of his intentions. These were difficult circumstances in the extreme, yet God's presence and comfort were nearer than ever.

People often criticise those who turn to God when the going gets difficult, and yet that is when he is particularly there for us, waiting with outstretched arms for us to throw ourselves into his embrace. Where else would we go?

Lord, thank you for the compassion you have shown at the times when my world has fallen apart. Help me extend that compassion to those around me who need your touch.

ALIE TEALE

Be honest in your dealings

There are those who turn justice into bitterness and cast
righteousness to the ground… There are those who hate the one
who upholds justice in court and detest the one who tells the truth.

I am happy to say that I have only ever been in court once and that was
to lend moral support to a group of people I know, not because I was
on trial. Nevertheless, being in court can be a scary experience. Eventually the case was thrown out of court because the plaintiffs could not
agree on their story, so the defendants were discharged.

Despite the tension, the whole experience was an interesting study
in what constitutes telling the truth. The problem about getting to the
truth of what happened in any situation is that each person involved
will have seen it from a different point of view—sometimes literally.
Maybe they were all standing in different places, or some of them had
their line of vision blocked for a while. Sometimes those points of view
are more subjective: one person is convinced they saw one thing and
another is just as sure they saw something different.

I am amazed at how much the human brain 'assumes' by filling in
the blanks in limited information. That innate ability helps us negotiate
our everyday lives, but when the chips are down and the truth must
come out, it can lead to considerable doubt. People can convince themselves that the way they wanted a situation to play out is what actually
happened.

The way we understand the truth should be through God's eyes,
even if we and those around us don't like what we see. How willing are
we to tell the truth and pursue justice even when it hurts, even when
we know it might make our lives difficult? I recently had to make a
truthful declaration on paper to the local court, even though I knew it
might cost me financially, but I firmly believe the Lord honours such
acts of integrity.

---

*'Who may ascend the mountain of the Lord? Who may stand in his holy
place? The one who has clean hands and a pure heart' (Psalm 24:3–4a).*
                                                                ALIE TEALE

Lazy fat cows

Hear this word, you cows of Bashan on Mount Samaria, you women who oppress the poor and crush the needy and say to your husbands, 'Bring us some drinks!' The Sovereign Lord has sworn by his holiness: '… You will each go straight out through breaches in the wall.'

Last Thursday we looked at Amos' criticism of the male leaders of Israel (the 'notable men'); now their wives are the target. Announcements of judgement are not politically correct; they criticise the status quo and use imagery to shock people out of their complacency. Amos doesn't hold back: he calls the leading women 'cows of Bashan on Mount Samaria'. Bashan (the Golan Heights) is still known for the well-fed cows that laze in the pastures chewing the cud, and it is these lazy, fat animals to which Amos compares the respected women of his time.

The term 'lazy cow' is still used in a derogatory way; I would be very insulted if someone called me that, especially if they added the adjective 'fat'! But are the times we live in much different from the time of Amos? After Christmas I was challenged about the cost of even a cheap bottle of wine. I had two supermarket-brand bottles left over after the festivities and I was running short of funds for food for the family. I decided to risk the humiliation of returning the bottles to the local supermarket, where I knew I might be able exchange them for something else. I came away with four loaves of bread, a French stick, eight pints of milk, four pints of fruit juice, ten bananas and some cheese. All that good healthy food in exchange for 150cl of mood-altering 'empty' calories that go straight to the hips!

Amos declares that women who indulge in excess at the expense of feeding those who are hungry will be thrown out through the holes in the walls with all the 'unmentionable waste' of the city. Maybe it's time to assess how much we have adopted the attitudes of the society we live in and change our ways?

Lord, forgive me for unthinkingly assimilating the debased values of the society in which I live. Show me the areas of my life in which I need to have self-discipline.

ALIE TEALE

Strongholds will crumble

'They do not know how to do right,' declares the Lord, 'who store up in their fortresses what they have plundered and looted.' Therefore this is what the Sovereign Lord says: 'An enemy will overrun your land, pull down your strongholds and plunder your fortresses.'

These verses from Amos are talking about the quantity of booty that the city of Ashdod and the country of Egypt have stored up from looting and plundering. This reminds me of the parable of the rich fool (Luke 12:13–21) who tears down his barns and builds bigger ones so that he can store his large harvest. The people in today's passage do not know how to do right, not only because they have taken what is not rightfully theirs but also because they have more than they require and do not have the heart to share it with those in need around them.

A couple of nights ago, I was in my local supermarket and saw quite a lot of loaves of bread that had been reduced in price by about 90 per cent so that the shop could clear them. I knew all these loaves could feed my family for weeks. The temptation to 'plunder' them all was strong, but I only took a few, because it seemed unfair to take them all when other people could benefit from them. The same went for the reduced-price yoghurt. Despite my innate greed (yes, let's call it what it really is!) I only took enough for the family's evening meal the next day.

I may not have a fortress full of treasure and I may not have a barn full of grain, but I do have two large freezers stuffed with food and I often wonder how I would feel if the electricity went off and they both defrosted or if someone broke in and took the contents. My 'barns' are my freezers; yours might be your wardrobes, china cabinets or bookshelves. How much stuff do we really need to store up against disaster when we could leave things for others and use what we have more beneficially?

Lord, help me to be on my guard against all kinds of greed and live with open hands, knowing that 'life does not consist in an abundance of possessions' (Luke 12:15).

ALIE TEALE

A famine for the word of God

'The days are coming... when I will send a famine through the land... a famine of hearing the words of the Lord. People will stagger from sea to sea and wander from north to east, searching for the word of the Lord, but they will not find it.'

This prophecy echoes the experience of the Israelites in the wilderness when they had nothing to eat or drink. God brought forth water from the rock and provided manna each morning so that they all had something to eat (Exodus 16:13—17:7). In Deuteronomy 8:3 we read that God did this so that his people would know that 'man does not live on bread alone but on every word that comes from the mouth of the Lord'.

Unfortunately, every generation seems to need to relearn the lessons recorded in the history books—or, in this case, the Bible. The people of Amos's time had forgotten that people need the word of the Lord to survive, so God was about to withhold his word further to make that very point.

The words of Amos were recorded partly so that we might learn from the mistakes the people made at that time, but have we done so? I meet a lot of young people and I am constantly amazed by their lack of knowledge of basic Bible stories, never mind the good news of salvation. Compared to the time of my youth, there is a famine of hearing the words of the Lord in our land. 'Lovely young women and strong young men... faint because of thirst' (v. 13), but do they 'stagger from sea to sea... searching for the word of the Lord' (v. 12)? I'm not sure they do. Perhaps they do not know what is missing in their lives to cause the deep spiritual craving and hunger that many of them must feel.

Can we relearn the sense of urgency in sharing the gospel and teaching people about Jesus that gripped the generation of preachers that preceded us? Or are we content to sit and let the waves of political correctness wash around us and say nothing?

'How, then, can they call on the one they have not believed in... [or] believe in the one of whom they have not heard... without someone preaching to them?' (Romans 10:14).

ALIE TEALE

Seek the Lord and live

'Seek me and live; do not seek Bethel, do not go to Gilgal, do not journey to Beersheba. For Gilgal will surely go into exile, and Bethel will be reduced to nothing.'

These verses speak to me of people who look for God in all the wrong places. Bethel (literally 'the house of God') was a religious centre in ancient Israel; Jacob had his dream of a ladder ascending to heaven there (Genesis 28:10–20) and Jeroboam set up two golden calves to be worshipped there, thus sinning against the Lord (1 Kings 12:25–30). Gilgal was the place where Joshua and the people of Israel settled on reaching the promised land (Joshua 4:19) and where Samuel anointed Saul as king and offered sacrifices (1 Samuel 10:8–10). God reiterated his covenant with Abraham to Isaac at Beersheba, and Isaac built an altar there and made a pact with King Abimelek (Genesis 26:23–33).

These places were all of immense historical, religious and political significance to key individuals and the people of Israel as a whole. Naturally people would have seen them as important and perhaps gravitated to them in times of trouble, but Amos announced that Bethel would be reduced to nothing and the inhabitants of Gilgal would be taken into exile.

When the chips are down, it doesn't matter where we might make pilgrimage or how significant we consider the place where we live to be, or how far we might try to run away from trouble—these things will not save us. The most important thing we can do every day of our lives is to 'seek the Lord and live'. We can seek and find God anywhere, any time and whatever the situation of our spiritual lives: 'If from there you seek the Lord your God, you will find him if you seek him with all your heart and with all your soul… For the Lord your God is a merciful God; he will not abandon or destroy you' (Deuteronomy 4:29, 31).

'Glory in his holy name; let the hearts of those who seek the Lord rejoice. Look to the Lord and his strength; seek his face always' (Psalm 105:3–4).
ALIE TEALE

God's promised blessing

'The days are coming,' declares the Lord, 'when the reaper will be overtaken by the ploughman and the planter by the one treading grapes. New wine will drip from the mountains and flow from all the hills, and I will bring my people Israel back from exile.'

After nine chapters of announcements of judgement, at last Amos brings us an announcement of salvation—a prophecy promising blessing from the hand of the Lord. However much doom and gloom a prophet proclaims, there is always light at the end of the tunnel, because the Lord does not want to execute judgement on those he loves.

As I mentioned earlier, the point of these announcements is to provoke change in a climate that is displeasing to God. They use extreme language to force people to examine their current spiritual and moral condition and decide to change. The more extreme the language, the greater the shock value and the more likely people are to allow the words to alter their frames of reference and thus their actions. Yet when God uses prophetic words to tear down an ideology that is causing people to behave in a way contrary to his best for us, there is always the promise of restoration and the building of something new that is in line with his way of being.

Amos's announcement of salvation uses metaphors from harvest to describe the abundance of the blessing that the Lord has in store for his people. Prophecy can be read at several levels: at face value, this prophecy speaks of the restoration of Israel after the return from exile, but, in the larger scheme of God's overarching plan for human history, we find here a marvellous description of the advancement of the kingdom of God after the coming of the Messiah.

Sowing and reaping are metaphors often used to describe people coming to faith, and new wine is a metaphor for the outpouring of the Holy Spirit. Wouldn't it be wonderful to see this massive sea-change that accelerates the coming of the kingdom of God in our own communities?

Lord, may we be part of the wonderful plan you have for humankind. May we be ready to be used by you, in the way you want and in the place where you have planted us.

ALIE TEALE

Making links

Annie Kirke writes:

John's Gospel is my favourite. The writer deliberately chooses aspects of stories that the other Gospels loosely touch on, or stories that are not mentioned at all elsewhere, to give us specific insights and truths concerning who Jesus is and what he came to do.

'In the beginning…' intentionally leads our minds back to Genesis 1, when God—the Father, Son and Spirit—began creating. Six days of creation climaxed in the creation of human beings in the image and likeness of God. God gave humankind *radah*—dominion on earth, as God has in heaven. Human beings are like royalty and are set apart to be a kingdom of priests (Exodus 19:6)—royal servants using their God-ordained power for good.

John's Gospel begins with the breathtaking announcement that Jesus, God in the flesh, has come among us. His humanity perfectly reveals what God intended for each of us in vocation, character and competency. John is carefully connecting Genesis 1's creation account with his own incarnation account. Jesus is the Word through whom creation and humankind came into being. Jesus, now among us, is the Word through whom creation and humankind are being recreated. At Pentecost the Spirit was poured out on everyone and the work of renewing creation was placed afresh in the hands of a Spirit-empowered humankind.

This Lent, I pray that you will take every opportunity to rediscover your true vocation as a royal priest in the kingdom of God. Take time away from distractions and diversions to be with God and allow his truth to liberate you and empower you to live in your true skin. The world is looking for signs that God exists. There is nothing more compelling than people who have been transformed by his Spirit.

The Bible verses quoted this week are taken from *The New Testament for Everyone* translated by Tom Wright (SPCK, 2011).

Word of life

In the beginning was the Word. The Word was close beside God, and the Word was God... Life was in him, and this life was the light of the human race. The light shines in the darkness, and the darkness didn't overcome it.

Whereas Matthew's Gospel begins by tracing Jesus' human genealogy back to Abraham (Matthew 1:1–16) and Luke takes it as far as 'son of Adam, son of God' (Luke 3:23–38), John begins even further back. As you read John 1:1–4 aloud, feel the full reality touch your heart, deepen your breathing and fill your spirit.

Many people today voice scientific and philosophical objections to the existence of a sovereign, all-loving, creator God; they believe that science, pain, suffering and natural and man-made disasters disprove God's existence. In 1936, Phyllis, aged six, wrote to Albert Einstein asking, 'Do scientists pray?' He replied, 'Everyone who is seriously involved in the pursuit of science becomes convinced that some spirit is manifest in the laws of the universe, one that is vastly superior to that of man.' Many scientists speak of this same discovery, which John 1:1–4 affirms and explains. This creative Spirit is not an impersonal force but a person—Jesus, who has now revealed himself to us.

In September 2012, I flew to Democratic Republic of Congo with a team to train 60 church leaders in inner healing prayer. Congo has the highest prevalence of rape in the world and has experienced decades of violence. Children are abducted and forced to fight with rebels. The area is called the 'heart of darkness' for good reason. However, when we arrived, we discovered something that the darkness had not overcome—light. Spirit-filled disciples were feeding, healing and supporting the hungry, destitute, sick, traumatised, widowed and orphaned. The darkness was palpably real but it could not overcome the light.

Disciples everywhere carry Jesus' transforming light and life. Where and to whom is God sending the Word of his life, healing and freedom through you today?

Jesus, please give me the words and courage to share this good news with others today.

ANNIE KIRKE

Word of truth

The Word became flesh and lived among us. We gazed upon his glory, glory like that of the father's only son, full of grace and truth.

Last winter, 280 churches offered shelter and hospitality to more than 1300 people sleeping out across 23 boroughs in the UK. 5200 volunteers cooked, washed up, listened, prayed, encouraged, played games and watched films with guests. These shelters became 'thin places'—a Celtic phrase for moments in time and place where Jesus is tangibly present, transforming lives.

At the Westminster Churches' night shelter, we have witnessed this transformation repeatedly. One guest arrived, having lived on the streets for years. The first evening, he came in with head down, eyes lowered. He was quiet and unresponsive to our welcome and the chatter of the other guests. He refused food, made a cup of coffee, got into his sleeping bag in the corner of the room and went to sleep. In the morning he sat away from the breakfast table, sipping coffee, and left without saying 'goodbye'. We could see how isolated his years on the street had made him, so we prayed and continued to be warm, friendly and welcoming while respecting his boundaries.

Over the following weeks, he began to change. He began making eye contact and responding to our 'hello's. He began eating with us, talking and playing games. On his last day with us, he stayed and helped me clear everything away while chatting excitedly about the flat that he was moving into the next day. He was a changed man.

Mindie Burgoyne writes in her blog 'Thin places', 'Truth abides in thin places; naked, raw, hard-to-face truth. Yet the comfort, safety and strength to face that truth also abides there' (www.thinplace.net). Babies experience their belovedness and a sense that all is well in the loving gaze of their mothers. Mothers are earthly mirrors of our belovedness to God. In God's gaze, we receive and know the deepest truth about ourselves.

Father, let me experience your loving gaze today.

ANNIE KIRKE

Spirit of freedom

I'm 'a voice calling in the desert,' he said. 'Straighten out the road for the master!'—just as the prophet Isaiah said… When you see the spirit coming down and resting on someone, that's the person who will baptise with the holy spirit. Well, that's what I saw, and I've given you my evidence: he is the son of God.'

The Gospel writer seems to assume that we already know about Jesus' baptism, so he focuses instead on its climax—the Holy Spirit coming and filling Jesus (vv. 32–34). We're told that this was the evidence that Jesus was God's Son, the one who would breathe God's Spirit into humankind, just as God did in Genesis 2:7. It was the beginning of God's renewal of creation.

I remember clearly the day I was filled with the Spirit. A friend had invited me to a prayer group where a man who had been a heroin addict for over a decade shared his story. He told us how his mum, a committed Christian, had prayed faithfully for him for years. One day, at his lowest point, he met some Christians who offered to pray for him. With nothing to lose, he agreed. As they prayed, a heat began to rise in his stomach. It intensified and a 'fire' went through his whole body. He described a liquid love coursing through him, which he knew was God's presence. He fell face down, convinced and overwhelmed by the experience. From that day he never took heroin again. The roots of the addiction were healed by the unconditional love of Jesus. These Christians invited him to live with them and he began his journey of transformation. When he asked if any of us would like to receive prayer too, I found my legs carrying me forward. I was not going to miss out!

Tomorrow, we follow Jesus, filled with the Spirit, into the desert to face and resist the root causes of our human frailty.

Thank you, Jesus, that your Spirit frees me from addictions and illusions. Strengthen me, this Lent, to resist lies and grow in the power of your Spirit.

ANNIE KIRKE

Sufficient for the day

Jesus returned from the Jordan, filled with the spirit. The spirit took him off into the wilderness for forty days, to be tested by the devil. He ate nothing during that time... 'If you are God's son,' said the devil, 'tell this stone to become a loaf of bread.' 'It is written,' replied Jesus, 'it takes more than bread to keep you alive.'

Imagine how Jesus felt after 40 days of fasting. At his weakest point, he was confronted with the temptations that Adam and Eve faced in the garden of Eden and Israel faced during their 40 years of wandering in the wilderness. Jesus quotes from a sermon given by Moses to the Israelites (see Deuteronomy 8:3), thus drawing parallels between their temptations and his. Will Jesus believe Satan's lies or will he reset humankind on God's intended course of implicit trust and obedience?

The first temptation Jesus faces is to choose self-sufficiency rather than dependency on God. He is hungry and the voice in his head is reminding him that he can easily make himself something to eat. What is he waiting for? Why is he denying himself? Jesus' response is clear: the people Israel were not kept alive just by the bread that God sent them each day but by his presence and his faithfulness. His word and promises sustained them. Jesus will not forfeit this dependency on God's timing and provision for a quick-fix meal made through his own means and resources.

I have a friend who has worked for three years with young people in gangs on a London estate. She has trusted God for her rent, food, travel, clothes and much-needed holidays. She has been consistently overwhelmed by God's kindness and perfect timing, but she has also struggled with the fear, anxieties and doubts that come with letting go and letting God provide. Each day she has to choose to become powerless in her own means, so that God can reveal his power. As a result, she has come to trust in God's love for her in ways that many Christians have not yet grasped because their need to control their own circumstances limits God.

Father, please show me where I am choosing self-sufficiency in my life rather than dependency on you. I choose you today!

ANNIE KIRKE

Power and authority

'It is written,' replied Jesus, '"The Lord your God is the one you must worship; he is the only one you must serve."'

In 1962, Nelson Mandela, a South African anti-apartheid lawyer and freedom fighter, was arrested and sentenced to life imprisonment on Robben Island. At his trial he gave an iconic speech in which he dedicated himself to opposing both white domination and black domination. He believed that a democratic and free society, in which all peoples could love harmoniously with equal opportunities, was possible and was a society that he was prepared to die for.

Mandela was released 27 years later. Old age, brutal prison labour, beatings and isolation had not quenched his cherished ideal. In 1992, aged 73, he became South Africa's first black president and the apartheid regime fell.

When God created human beings in his image and gave them authority over the earth, he established a power-sharing relationship with us through which we would promote and achieve personal, social and economic well-being, security and human flourishing for all creation, as God intends.

However, at the fall, we rejected relationship with God, seeking equality with God in status and power. We became corrupted by the power that God had given us, using it for our own gains and to manipulate and dominate others. Mandela is a rare example of a leader who chose not to misuse his presidency: he could have punished white South Africans for their years of oppressive behaviour, but instead he promoted peace and reconciliation.

In Luke 4:5–8, we discover that Jesus faced the same temptation to idolise both himself and power. However, Jesus 'did not consider equality with God something to be used to his own advantage' (see Philippians 2:6, NIV) and disarmed the lie with scripture. He came to serve the Father and use his power for the good of others, as God intends that we should.

Jesus, show me how I can serve you and others with the natural and supernatural power you give me.

ANNIE KIRKE

Faithful one

Then the devil took him to Jerusalem, and stood him on a pinnacle of the Temple. 'If you are God's son,' he said, 'throw yourself down from here...' 'It has been said,' replied Jesus, '"You mustn't put the Lord your God to the test."'

God raised up Moses to take the Israelites out of Egypt after their 400 years in captivity there, but it took God another 40 years to take Egypt out of the Israelites.

First, the Israelites emerged from Egypt with an orphan mindset. God spent 40 years teaching them to trust in his *hesed* love—his covenantal faithfulness, love and compassion towards them. In return, God required the Israelites simply to be faithful to him, but they were repeatedly childish, disobedient and unfaithful, treating God like a slot-machine rather than cherishing their unique relationship with him.

Second, the people emerged with a poverty mindset. They moaned, quarrelled and rebelled, no matter what God provided for them. The Israelites struggled to find rest in God because they lived for his presents rather than his presence. They pestered Moses to persuade God to give them the land he had promised Abraham, while denying the conditions of faithfulness that God had attached to their receipt of it.

Finally, the Israelites emerged with an idolatrous mindset. While Moses was up on Mount Sinai receiving the ten commandments, the people built a golden calf (an Egyptian idol) to worship and petition for their needs.

The Israelites struggled to trust God's covenant of faithfulness, compassion and provision for them. In our passage today, we see just the opposite in Jesus, who is confident and fully trusting of his Father God. He knows his Father, so is no orphan. He knows that God will provide for him, so he has no fear of poverty or want. He focuses on God's will and word, so is not persuaded to listen to the distraction of the enemy.

When we feel pain, anxiety or fear, in what ways do we turn to people, distractions or addictions rather than God for our consolation or remedy?

ANNIE KIRKE

Spiritual opportunities

The spirit of the Lord is upon me because he has anointed me to tell the poor the good news. He has sent me to announce release to the prisoners and sight to the blind, to set the wounded victims free, to announce the year of God's special favour.

Having faced and overcome the same temptations that Adam and Eve and Israel faced as God's chosen people, Jesus emerges from his time in the wilderness empowered by the Spirit to do the will and work of the Father in bringing forgiveness, healing, deliverance and resurrection life to others.

The Father, Son and Holy Spirit are at work again now, making new creation from within the old creation. When we face a time of testing and temptation, it often precedes new spiritual opportunities to serve God in the world and to experience the Holy Spirit moving more powerfully in and through us. Rather than seeing the tests as a sign of weakness or even failure, we can learn to see them as a sign of opportunity, growth and maturity. If Jesus grew in wisdom, spiritual power and discernment by overcoming temptation and trials, then so can we.

After his announcement that the kingdom was arriving, Jesus called his first disciples to follow him (Luke 5). In doing so, he revealed how the kingdom life is seen by and extended to others—through a community of obedient followers who increasingly share in his character and competencies. He also revealed that kingdom leadership is a team effort, not a one-(wo)man show. At first, the disciples watched and learned, but then Jesus sent them out in pairs to find people who were open to them and receptive to the gospel, who would willingly invite them into their social circles to share the good news about the kingdom, heal the sick and cast out demons (Luke 10). This was how the gospel spread through the region.

Imagine that Jesus wants to share the gospel, through you, with your community, office or social group. Who could you pair up with to begin praying and serving together?

ANNIE KIRKE

Making links

Jill Rattle writes:

The last letter written by someone shortly before their death to someone they love dearly is bound to be heartfelt, poignant and important to both of them.

Paul is in a prison cell and he knows that his earthly days are numbered. He has been nurturing Timothy in the faith and preparing him for Christian leadership when Paul will no longer be around to support and mentor him. They have become very close, and the letter we know as 2 Timothy must have been hard to write and hard to receive. There is a note of urgency about it: there is so little time left.

Everything Paul writes is to encourage Timothy to persevere in sharing the gospel, to keep going in the tough times (including times of persecution) and to stay faithful to Jesus. Paul stresses that Timothy must be faithful both in his ministry and in his conduct: his life and behaviour must bear witness to the truth of what he teaches. He urges Timothy to immerse himself in the scriptures, which will provide him with all the guidance he needs. He gives Timothy some strong warnings about the dangers and temptations that might hinder his ministry and urges him to 'fan into flame the gift of God' given to him through the laying on of Paul's hands.

Paul expresses his thankfulness for Timothy's love, reveals how often he prays for him and begs him to come quickly and visit him one last time. Sadly, it seems that a number of Paul's erstwhile supporters have abandoned him to his fate, but Timothy remains loyal. Despite the desperate nature of his circumstances, Paul declares confidently that his Saviour 'will bring me safely to his heavenly kingdom'.

Wonderful women

I am reminded of your sincere faith, which first lived in your grandmother Lois and in your mother Eunice and, I am persuaded, now lives in you also.

There is an amazing number of Christians, both young and old, in my extended family—far more than you might expect. Sometimes I wonder if, generations back, there was a woman who prayed day by day, year by year, for her children and her children's children, and here in 2015 we are still seeing the answers to her prayers. Certainly both my grandmothers were faithful pray-ers.

Timothy was similarly blessed. Grandma Lois taught daughter Eunice about Jesus, and Eunice did the same for her son Timothy. Timothy, though, did not inherit the life of Jesus from them: he had to come to Jesus himself and choose to be his disciple. I'm sure Lois and Eunice were thrilled when he did, and I'm also sure they didn't give up praying. What a joy for them to see Timothy becoming a mature Christian and a church leader!

I still remember the day when I realised that just because Mum and Dad were Christians, it didn't mean I was one. Like Timothy, I chose for myself to follow Jesus and my parents were as thrilled as Lois and Eunice must have been.

Perhaps you are among those whose families have no Christian belief, but the fact that you are reading this suggests you are a follower of Jesus and seeking to be his disciple. I'm sure you are well aware of the privilege and responsibility of praying for those close to you. Just think, you may be the one whose faithful prayers have a great influence on friends, family and colleagues now and for generations yet to come. The Holy Spirit will take your prayers and do something amazing with them. Lois and Eunice were wonderful women and, as far as the Holy Spirit is concerned, so are you.

Ask the Holy Spirit to direct your mind to a child or young person belonging to your or a friend's family, and commit to praying for them regularly.

JILL RATTLE

Not suffering alone

Join with me in suffering for the gospel, by the power of God. He has saved us and called us to a holy life—not because of anything we have done but because of his own purpose and grace.

Many teachers now assess pupils' work using something called 'two stars and a wish'—two good points and one thing they wish the child had done better. I recently heard of a particular boy who handed in an RE essay. His teacher was amazed: the boy had never submitted homework before. The teacher duly marked the essay and wrote, 'Two stars: first one for handing it in, the second for good sentences and punctuation. The wish: that you had read the title correctly and written about suffering, not surfing!'

I must admit, there does sometimes seem to be more suffering in our Christian lives than surfing, more struggle than fun. Do you find that? Paul writes to Timothy as if it is normal for Jesus' followers to face tough times. Life, as many of us can attest, does not become easier when we become Christians; it often becomes harder as we try to live out the gospel. Paul suggests that this 'suffering' is something that binds us together with other believers. We all have tough times: we all need each other's support, prayer, love and ministry. We don't just have each other, though. Look again at Paul's words quoted above: 'Join me in suffering for the gospel, by the power of God.' At every moment, in every circumstance, the power of God is available to the believer—the power to protect, the power to heal, the power to transform.

Jesus does not send us suffering. He does not like us to suffer, but in a broken world he cannot remove all the rough experiences from us. He does promise, however, to accompany us on each step of the hard path and to transform our experience by his love. God will 'never leave you nor forsake you' (Deuteronomy 31:6).

Lord, help me to be aware of your love in both the good times and the tough times. May I be faithful to you and your gospel at all times.

JILL RATTLE

The mentor

What you heard from me, keep as the pattern of sound teaching, with faith and love in Christ Jesus.

Recently I asked my grandchildren, aged 9 and 6, what advice I have given them that they remember. 'Chew! Chew! Chew!' they shot back. Hmm. Well, it's sound advice for eating your food at meal times, but not quite what I'd hoped to hear.

Paul's advice to his young protégé, Timothy, is on a higher level altogether. This letter from Paul is full of important truths and principles for Timothy to grasp as he emerges as a leader of the growing Christian church.

I wonder how easy Timothy found it to absorb all the advice Paul offered. Sometimes, advice, even if it's well meant, can be unhelpful. In the Old Testament, Job's 'comforters' are a case in point: they had an awful lot of advice to offer, some of it sounding very theologically correct, but it was the wrong advice at the wrong time, given in the wrong way.

That is not the case here with Paul and Timothy. Why am I sure of that? Look back at chapter 1, where Paul writes, 'Night and day I constantly remember you in my prayers' (v. 3). Before Paul offered a word of advice, he had been praying regularly for Timothy, listening for the Spirit's prompting. Consequently, what Paul had to say was what Timothy needed to hear. It was advice that would help Timothy to 'pursue righteousness, faith, love and peace' (2:22).

It seems to me that praying before we offer advice to others is a very good principle to adopt. Let's talk to God before we speak, and trust the Holy Spirit to give us the right words—words that will encourage, not discourage; words that build up and don't knock down.

We need more mentors like Paul in the fellowship of the church. Perhaps you could be one?

Prayerfully consider whether you might offer to mentor someone. Could you yourself benefit from having a mentor who would encourage and support you?

JILL RATTLE

Soldier, athlete, farmer

No one serving as a soldier gets entangled in civilian affairs... an athlete does not receive the victor's crown except by competing according to the rules. The hardworking farmer should be the first to receive a share of the crops.

I must admit that comparing myself with a soldier, athlete or farmer does not come easily: I don't like doing as I'm told, my idea of physical fitness is a chocolate bar after a spa jacuzzi, and digging ditches or mucking out cows is a definite no-no. However, Paul tells Timothy that the Lord has a message in these pictures for him—and, presumably, for you and me.

The qualities shared by the soldier, athlete and farmer are commitment, discipline and hard work. As a result, the soldier is commended by his commanding officer, the athlete wins a medal and the farmer enjoys a great harvest.

How does this apply to me as a Christian? If I'm serious about committing myself to Jesus, he will give me tasks to help him build his kingdom of love and justice. Those tasks will need commitment, discipline and hard work. In Ephesians 2:10 we read, 'For we are God's handiwork, created in Christ Jesus to do good works, which God prepared in advance for us to do.' I love that last phrase. God has already done the groundwork for the jobs he wants us to do. It's a partnership with him, which makes the commitment, discipline and hard work seem a lot less daunting. The rewards are great—among them are joy, love and peace.

It's not always easy to discover what our specific kingdom tasks are, but, as we pray and read the scriptures, the Holy Spirit will show us. Then, thankfully, he will give us the necessary strength, wisdom and skills.

We do not earn God's favour by accomplishing certain tasks—he loves us just as much when we're lazy or ineffective—but he is delighted when we choose to cooperate with him in building his kingdom.

Come, Holy Spirit, and show me those things you have prepared in advance for me to do. For your kingdom's sake. Amen

JILL RATTLE

Goblet or waste bin?

Those who cleanse themselves.... will be instruments for special purposes, made holy, useful to the Master and prepared to do any good work.

Have you played that (dangerous!) game where you liken people to various animals? Perhaps your daughter is a gazelle, your best friend is a labrador and your boss is a duck-billed platypus...

Paul asks Timothy to liken himself not to an animal but to a kitchen utensil. 'Which kitchen utensil do you want to be?' he asks, listing some: 'crystal goblets and silver platters... waste cans and compost buckets—some containers used to serve fine meals, others to take out the garbage' (v. 20, THE MESSAGE). I'm sure Timothy knew exactly which utensil he wanted to be. I do: I would love to be a crystal goblet or silver platter in God's kitchen, or even, at a push, one of those nice shiny aluminium waste disposal units. If I'm honest, though, I sometimes feel more like the slightly grubby plastic swing-bin hidden under the sink.

Paul urges Timothy to be the sort of special container that is fit for God's holy purposes and gives him examples of some of the behaviours he needs to avoid if he is to be 'clean' and live a godly life that God can use to bless others. These behaviours include 'godless chatter', childish indulgence, hypocrisy, being argumentative and quarrelsome (especially over minor theological differences) and resentment. How do we get ourselves that clean?

To a degree, the clean-up process to fit us for God's purposes is down to us: we need to make conscious choices to avoid those situations and behaviours that hinder our usefulness. Thankfully, though, God does not leave us to do all the cleaning ourselves. The Holy Spirit gently but firmly shows us the grubby bits in our lives and, as we confess and repent of them, gives us the forgiveness we need and the strength to do better.

Lord, only you can transform me into a crystal goblet. Please make me useful in your service.

JILL RATTLE

2 TIMOTHY 3 (NIV)

Dark and light

People will be lovers of themselves, lovers of money, boastful,
proud, abusive, disobedient to their parents, ungrateful, unholy,
without love, unforgiving, slanderous, without self-control, brutal,
not lovers of the good, treacherous, rash, conceited, lovers of
pleasure rather than lovers of God.

In this passage, Paul starts by sketching an unpleasant picture of people
in 'the last days'. It reads like a preliminary outline for another 'Nordic
noir' TV thriller series—black as black can be. The sad thing is that we
can see examples of this ugliness in every newspaper, every TV broad-
cast, across the internet and, sometimes, with our own eyes. We live in
a world that seems more broken by the day.

Even so, amid the gathering darkness there are countless points of
light. There are human acts of kindness—care for a neighbour, feeding the hungry, reaching out to the refugee; human acts of courage—
defending the weak, opposing the dictator, rescuing those in danger;
and human acts of integrity—speaking unpopular truths, fighting corruption, seeking justice.

It's not just Christians who, day by day, demonstrate love, justice
and peace. Millions of people, made in the image of God but not yet
acknowledging the source of their goodness, try to be light in dark
places. I once heard a speaker say that many people, if not most people,
have their faces turned in the direction of the kingdom of God. It is the
task of those of us who call ourselves Christians to point them onward
to Jesus, the light of the world.

Paul calls Timothy to this task and reminds him that he will find
the wisdom, strength and knowledge to do it through the scriptures,
'which are able to make you wise for salvation through faith in Christ
Jesus' (v. 15). More than that, everything we need to know is there: 'All
Scripture is God-breathed and is useful for teaching, rebuking, correct-
ing and training in righteousness, so that the servant of God may be
thoroughly equipped for every good work' (vv. 16–17).

---

*Lord, we pray that the church may become more effective in spreading
the light of Jesus through the nations. Please equip me for my part.*

JILL RATTLE

The end and the beginning

The time for my departure is near. I have fought the good fight, I have finished the race, I have kept the faith.

The email came as no surprise but it still made me sad. My former pastor, now in his 80s, was writing to say he was in the terminal stage of cancer. So many memories of his kindness, integrity and faithful service came flooding in. What a good race he has run!

Timothy must have felt sad to read Paul's assertion that his life was about to end—not a natural death, but a martyrdom. Timothy would lose his mentor, his friend, the one who had encouraged his gifts and prepared him for leadership, but Paul was ready to move on to the great adventure. His marathon was over and ahead lay the wonder of meeting Jesus face to face and receiving from him the 'crown of righteousness' (v. 8). In that moment, Paul would be made perfect and new. He couldn't wait!

But then Timothy reads, 'When you come, bring the cloak that I left with Carpus at Troas, and my scrolls, especially the parchments.' I love the reality of that request. Heaven awaits, but Paul needs the coat he left behind and his manuscripts—because he's planning to go on serving God until the very end and his cell is a bit chilly.

In his email, my former pastor asked for prayer that he would have the strength to complete whatever work the Lord had for him to do in the time he had left. He wanted to be faithful to the end.

When Paul has departed, Timothy and his fellow Christians will carry on the mission to present Jesus to the world. From them the good news comes down the generations, and now it's in our hands. We have our work to complete, our race to run—and God will give us the strength, the direction and the time to do it.

Come, Holy Spirit! Help me to run my race well, keeping my eyes fixed on Jesus.

JILL RATTLE

Prayer focus

On 26 February, Jill asked us to think about Paul's image of the kitchen utensil (or, in other translations, any household implement).

If you would like to dwell on these thoughts a little longer, go into your kitchen and take a good look around. What are your most useful, well-used items? Which gadgets do you bring out only on special occasions? Which of these tools are all-purpose and which are specialised for a particular task? Are there some pieces that are not especially useful but are none the less treasured for their decorative beauty or the memories they bring back?

Do you have items pushed to the back of a cupboard that never see the light of day—or even a 'rubbish' drawer crammed with broken bits and bobs that really don't have a job to do any longer?

What matters most about any of these utensils, in all their amazing variety, is that they are clean and fit for their own purpose.

In prayer, ask God if there is anything he wants to say to you in relation to one or more of your kitchen utensils. What sort of function is he calling you to? Are you willing to be used by him in this way? Are you 'clean and fit for purpose'?

If you keep a journal, note down anything significant that comes to mind as a result of this exercise.

LISA CHERRETT

Making links

Jean Watson writes:

For a long time now, I have been passionate about genuineness and self-honesty. I think life's painful and difficult experiences often reveal—in ourselves and others—what doesn't ring true and hasn't stood the test of time. In these two weeks of notes, I look at getting real about 14 aspects of our lives in our humanness and our Christianity. I believe that 'truth in the inward being' (Psalm 51:6, NRSV) is what God wants from us and what sets us free. However, truth on its own or delivered coldly can be very painful, off-putting or even destructive. Truth from God, who is the ultimate reality and the source of all truth, always comes with love, because God *is* love, so we need not fear it or run from it. Let me encourage you, then, to get real with me.

'Hiding'
I go to St Sound—the popular church—
but am I really one of them:
they so secure—I so adrift;
they so sorted—and I so sore;
they so together—I so makeshift;
so bespoke while they ignore
my silence or shy questioning?
So I am hiding much of who
and where I truly am. And you
perhaps? Now there's a startling thought!
How many of us might there be
who feel the same? Integrity
from inside out should be the deal.
But truth's a dagger if not sheathed
with understanding empathy;
fear of rejection fosters fakes
while a starred love sets people free
to shed our masks, be real,
for God's and all our sakes.

Getting real about faith

[Thomas] said to them, 'Unless I see the nail marks... I will not believe.'... Thomas said to him, 'My Lord and my God!'

Thomas, in today's Bible passage, was being totally real in his faith and his relationship with Jesus. He doubted what he had been told and was honest about it: he didn't pretend. He said, in effect, 'I want proof.'

Thomas was given proof and his immediate willingness to accept it and respond to it in the way that he did shows us that his doubt was genuine, neither an excuse nor a smokescreen.

I admire Thomas for his honesty about his doubt. It gives me permission to be honest about mine. What about you? Do you sometimes doubt and are you honest about it, or do you have an unwavering faith? If, like me, you are prone to doubt at times, you may find the theologian Jack Dominian's words helpful: 'We live between faith and doubt, which can only be bridged by love.'

Not until we meet Jesus face to face will we have the kind of proof that Thomas wanted and received, but we can be open to him, turning to him in prayer with our doubts and our weak or small faith. Even if we do not receive the answer we want, we can be in his presence and receive his love, which will lift our spirits and warm our hearts. I call such experiences 'Ah' moments or, as Celtic Christians described them, 'thin places'. They can occur as we read a book, talk with a friend, listen to music, meditate on scripture or enjoy or reflect on God's creativity.

'I do believe; help me overcome my unbelief!' (Mark 9:24). 'The apostles said to the Lord, "Increase our faith!"' (Luke 17:5).

JEAN WATSON

Getting real about myself

'First take the plank out of your eye, and then you will see clearly to remove the speck from the other person's eye.'

Our verses for today emphasise the need for self-honesty, for 'truth in the inward being'. Jesus asks how we can ignore a plank in our own eye while pointing critically to the speck in someone else's. This prompts me to ask, 'Who am I in reality? In my inner being? In my heart? Does what I criticise or dislike in others clue me in to some unpalatable truth about myself?'

Someone once said something like this to me: 'I don't think about myself, I just focus on other people.' This sounds very laudable but, if I am totally unaware of who I am, of my inside story, I am not likely to be insightful about or sensitive towards another person. Narcissistic navel-gazing won't equip me for helping people either, but I do need to know who I am on the inside, to have brought out into the light and made peace with my inside story, including any hidden secrets. Only then will I have the 'space' and the tranquillity to be truly hospitable or helpful to anyone else.

Personality tests and opening up to a trusted friend can help us to get real about ourselves; reading good biographies and novels is another excellent way of finding out more about how we and other people 'tick'. Anything that challenges or nudges us into making time for quiet reflection on these matters is beneficial. Why not, for a week or more, take time at the end of each day to look back over what has happened and over your responses and emotions, by asking questions such as 'What energised or dispirited me today? What pleased or saddened me? What delighted or irritated me?'

'Above all else, guard your heart, for everything you do flows from it' (Proverbs 4:23, NIV).

JEAN WATSON

Getting real about grace

It is by grace you have been saved, through faith—and this is not
from yourselves, it is the gift of God.

'Grace' is not a word used in common parlance and it doesn't mean
much to most people. Even some churchgoers would be hard pressed
to define the word clearly. The dictionary uses words like 'attractive-
ness, favour and mercy' to define 'grace' and indicates that it involves
both attitude and actions.

Ephesians 2 tells us that we have been saved by grace. This salvation
comes from Jesus who, 'in his kindness' (v. 7), forgives us and raises us
to true spiritual life and riches 'even when we were dead in transgressions' (v. 5). This chimes with the familiar mnemonic that grace means
'Great Riches At Christ's Expense'.

Although this grace is freely given, it surely prompts a response. We
need to receive it with thankfulness and learn to grow in our ability
to reflect something of it to others. In the parable of the unmerciful
servant (Matthew 18:21–35), the servant whose master forgave him for
the 10,000 bags of gold he owed, but who then didn't cancel the 100
silver coins that someone else owed him, was sternly reprimanded and
punished. The master asked, 'Shouldn't you have had mercy on your
fellow servant just as I had on you?' to which the answer is, colloquially
speaking, a no-brainer!

Aware of the grace we have been (and are continually) shown, we
need to show grace and to 'grow in grace' (2 Peter 3:18), which means
to become more merciful, forgiving and kind. It's quite easy to be like
that to people we like, who are good to us, but I guess we all need
God's help to reflect his kind of grace to the 'undeserving'—those who
are not kind, or are even positively unkind, to us.

---

*Bask in the reflection that God's grace is amazing—even more so because
he does not see us as 'wretches' but as 'beloved'. Can you see others like
this, at least potentially?*

JEAN WATSON

Getting real about suffering

We are hard pressed on every side, but not crushed; perplexed, but not in despair; persecuted, but not abandoned; struck down, but not destroyed… Therefore we do not lose heart… For our light and momentary troubles are achieving for us an eternal glory that far outweighs them all.

Scripture doesn't tell us that suffering shouldn't happen to Christians or that a lack of faith, prayer or discernment causes it to happen. This untheological and unreal thinking causes a great deal of unnecessary suffering.

THE MESSAGE paraphrases 2 Corinthians 4:8–9 like this:

We've been surrounded and battered by troubles, but we're not demoralised; we're not sure what to do, but we know that God knows what to do; we've been spiritually terrorised, but God hasn't left our side; we've been thrown down, but we haven't broken.

Getting real about suffering doesn't mean believing that God doesn't care and isn't involved in our lives. Many Bible passages tell us that he does and is. As we trust in his presence, his promises and his provision for our wonderful future, he will be with us in our dark experiences in the present and in the glorious and wonderful life to come in our eternal future.

We can come to the Lord each and every day with the struggles we face. As it says in 2 Corinthians 4:16, 'Inwardly we are being renewed day by day', and he will give us the strength to carry on. Jesus said, 'In this world you will have trouble'. He added, 'But take heart! I have overcome the world' (John 16:33).

'God… comforts us in all our troubles, so that we can comfort those in any trouble' (2 Corinthians 1:3–4).

JEAN WATSON

Getting real about blessings

'The God who made the world and everything in it… gives everyone life and breath and everything else.'

These words from Acts 17 talk about the physical blessings that God gives us. Ephesians 1:3–10 tells us that God has blessed us also 'with every spiritual blessing in Christ'. Those blessings include redemption and grace in this life, followed by the life to come when Jesus will be Lord over the new heaven and the new earth.

Because of my temperament and because of things that have happened in my life, I am visited by two enemies of peace and joy—anxiety and fear. Finding ways of dealing with them is an ongoing learning experience. Medication and counselling can be part of God's provision for those who are disabled by fear and anxiety, but one of the other ways in which I try to counter my low days is to get real about my blessings. I need to name them, be thankful for them and make the most of them. For example, I might ring or call on a friend, choose to start doing something different, energising, creative or enjoyable, or reflect on my spiritual blessings.

Can you make a mental or written list of your physical, material and spiritual blessings? Psalm 104, if you have time to glance through it, will give you many ideas to add to your lists.

John O'Donohue, in his book *Benedictus* (Bantam, 2007), identifies some of the blessings that can so easily be taken for granted, including friendship, health and 'the ability to see, to hear, to understand and to celebrate life'. Right at the top of my list of blessings I have those whom I love and those who love me, and these include—incredibly, I sometimes feel—'the God who made the world and everything in it', the God who 'is love' (1 John 4:8).

Reflect on your blessings and delight in the love behind the gifts.

JEAN WATSON

Getting real about love

Love... always protects, always trusts, always hopes, always perseveres.

1 Corinthians 13 is a passage that I love and come back to again and again, as it spells out how 'many-splendoured ' love is and what it looks like in action. You might like to ponder this, summarise the passage in your own words and/or cite your own examples of what love is like and does. I also love 1 John 4:16: 'God is love. Whoever lives in love lives in God, and God in them '

Among many other things, love helps us to get real. Many of you will know the famous quotation about love and reality in the children's book by Margery Williams called *The Velveteen Rabbit*: 'When a child loves you for a long, long time, not just to play with, but REALLY loves you, then you become Real.'

I always hope to be reassured that God loves me and welcomes me just as I am *before* I am reminded (whether I need such a reminder or not) that I am a miserable sinner who needs to confess my sins. It is only in the context of being loved that I feel secure and non-defensive enough to admit my faults and weaknesses, and I don't think I am alone in this regard.

That said, getting real about real love involves admitting our failures in love; it involves also being willing to work at getting better at loving and being realistic about the self-discipline required and the potential pain that we risk when we choose to love. Like Aslan in the 'Narnia Chronicles' by C.S. Lewis, real love is not safe, but it is good. In fact, it is wonderful, and it's what makes real life really worth living.

Love is such a risk, Lord, but help me to take the risk of loving even if I have been badly hurt by loss or betrayal. As I get real about love, may I experience and reflect it more and more and better and better.

JEAN WATSON

Getting real about prayer (1)

Jesus went out to a mountainside to pray, and spent the night praying to God.

Jesus was real about prayer. Luke 6 speaks of him going out alone on a mountain and praying all night; in the morning, resourced and guided, he chose the twelve apostles. Many other incidents in Jesus' life illustrate how real he was about prayer to God.

After some traumas in my life, I found I needed to get real about my prayer life and make changes. What follows is not a blueprint for anyone else—just an outline of how I tried to do it, as a possible encouragement to others.

I found that praying with lots of people for lots of things—one after the other—didn't feel all that real and helpful for me personally. I seemed to need some silence after each prayer to take it in and echo a genuine 'Amen—so be it', as well as to think about what I might want to pray for.

I continued going to a small prayer group that has been running for many years and is a great source of strength to the members. We meet weekly to pray for and support one another and others through times of trouble and loss—and to rejoice together in times of joy.

I became part of another, even smaller prayer group, which meets to pray for people from local churches who are doing the work of befrienders in the community.

I also pray with and for those who come to me on a one-to-one basis to talk about their spiritual life and journey.

In my private prayer, I have always been drawn to intercessory prayer—naming the people whose lives touch mine in any way—but I need and want to learn more about 'practising the presence of God' and to find more time for meditation.

Think in God's presence about how real you are about and in prayer.

JEAN WATSON

Getting real about prayer (2)

Pray in the Spirit on all occasions with all kinds of prayers and requests. With this in mind, be alert and always keep on praying for all the Lord's people. Pray also for me, that whenever I speak, words may be given me.

Using a concordance and looking up some of the many references to prayer, I find that people in the Bible prayed in all sorts of emotional and geographical situations, and about a wide variety of people and issues. The message I get from that, and from Ephesians 6:18–20 (our passage for today) is that we can pray about anything, at any time and in any place.

I have been reading through the Psalms and one thing that has struck me is the way the psalmists pour out their hearts to God very honestly about who and where they are at the time. They certainly give us permission to do the same—to get real in prayer to God.

The last present given to me by one of our small prayer group before she died of cancer was a notebook in which, in her memory, I started to write down some of my very honest prayers at that time. I'd like to share one of these prayers, to encourage you to open up honestly to God about something:

They sing, 'You alone are my heart's desire.' But you are not—not alone. My heart also desires human cherishing; desires my loved ones' flourishing. What does that make me? Guilty? Ungrateful? A third-rate saint? Or real about all you provide anonymously, unsigned, for us, your creatures—corporeal, physical as well as inspired, inspirited.

Lord, I want to pour out my heart to you about...

JEAN WATSON

Getting real about God's provision

[Jesus said] 'If that is how God clothes the grass of the field, which is here today and tomorrow is thrown into the fire, will he not much more clothe you—you of little faith?'

In Matthew 6:25–30, Jesus tells his followers not to worry about things such as food and drink, because God will meet those needs for them. But how does he meet those physical needs for us—and what about our spiritual and psychological needs?

In 1 Corinthians 12:24–31, Paul gives us a picture of the body with all the parts being necessary and having a vital role to play; and of God giving different gifts to different people for the good of all. He says, 'There should be no division in the body, but… its parts should have equal concern for each other' (v. 25).

What are we to make of all this? I take it to mean that, ultimately, God does provide for all our needs by everything that he has created and sustains. But the way he meets our needs—physical, psychological and spiritual—is through one another as we make use of and share his gifts.

I've made a list of everything I think I need for my health and well-being and, alongside, I've named the people or agencies (human and divine) by which those needs are being met. There are about 13 items in each of my lists. Perhaps, now or at another time, you would like to make similar lists about your needs. If you discover that some of your needs are not being met, you might like to think about why this is so. Is God's provision lacking or is it that human beings are not playing a full part in the process?

Help me to get real about my needs and to show appreciation towards all those who are meeting them. For all that you provide, thank you, Father, Son and Holy Spirit.

JEAN WATSON

Getting real about lifestyle

'Is not this the kind of fasting I have chosen: to loose the chains of injustice… to share your food with the hungry and to provide the poor wanderer with shelter?'

This passage in Isaiah is very specific about the kind of lifestyle God wants his people to have. It should involve taking action against injustice, freeing the oppressed, sharing food with the hungry, giving shelter to the homeless and clothing the naked. As the letter of James says, 'Faith by itself, if it is not accompanied by action, is dead' (2:17).

Jesus identified himself with this type of ministry (Luke 4:18–19) and the apostle John asks how God's love can possibly be in us if we don't share our possessions with people in need around us (1 John 3:16–18).

It's easy to think that injustice, inequality and poverty are such massive issues that we can't do anything about them. Ruth Valerio has written a book called *L is for Lifestyle: Christian living that doesn't cost the earth* (IVP, 2004), which helps us to see how everyone can make step-changes towards creating a more Christian, godly lifestyle that will contribute to building a fairer world for everyone.

We can all recycle and try to buy as much Fairtrade, locally grown and seasonal food as we can. We can support, financially and in prayer, at least one of the many organisations whose aims are in keeping with today's passages and others that are similar in the Bible. These are just a few of the 101 suggestions in Ruth's book about loving our world and our neighbour for God's and all our sakes.

Reflect on 1 John 3:16–18 and pray: Jesus, God with us, help me to think about my lifestyle in the light of your character and priorities.

JEAN WATSON

Getting real about discipleship

'Come, follow me,' Jesus said, 'and I will send you out to fish for people.'

What does being a disciple of Jesus really mean and entail? The short answer to both parts of that question is 'following Jesus', but Jesus made other statements about discipleship. I'd like to think about three of them.

'Whoever wants to be my disciple must deny themselves and take up their cross and follow me' (Mark 8:34). This is one of the many verses in the Bible that mustn't be taken literally; rather, its meaning must be properly interpreted and understood. A true disciple of Jesus must place Jesus, not self, at the centre of his or her life and be prepared to face suffering. This is not to be interpreted as 'Being Jesus' disciple means having low self-esteem and finding life to be grim and joyless all the time.' Jesus' own life refutes this distortion. He was accused by some not just of mixing with the wrong people but also of having rather too good a time. Of course, he also experienced opposition and injustice, as well as death at a young age, but he was a man who enjoyed people and lived life to the full—even before his resurrection.

'If anyone comes to me and does not hate father and mother, wife and children, brothers and sisters—yes, even their own life—such a person cannot be my disciple' (Luke 14:26). Again, this cannot be taken literally, since Jesus did not hate his family but respected and cared for them. He was using typical and well-understood Jewish hyperbole (exaggeration). The meaning is again about priorities. Jesus must come first in our lives and priorities—not always an easy option.

'If you hold to my teaching, you are really my disciples' (John 8:31). This must mean that following Jesus includes putting his teaching into practice in our lives.

Reflect on and pray about any aspect of discipleship that you are struggling with.

JEAN WATSON

Getting real about heaven

Then I saw 'a new heaven and a new earth', for the first heaven and the first earth had passed away.

Getting real about heaven, it seems to me, means admitting that we know very little about it. We know that there will be a new heaven and new earth, and this is where God and his people will ultimately and eternally be, with 'no more death or mourning or crying or pain' (v. 4).

That said, there's a lot we don't know about heaven. Once, when my small son asked me, 'Where is heaven?' I began trying to answer the question, but he interrupted and said, 'I'll ask Granny. She's better at directions!' Clearly, my attempt at an explanation hadn't been satisfactory, which is hardly surprising, because heaven's whereabouts are way beyond our understanding and our language—or, at least, beyond mine. The question 'When do we get there?' is not much easier to answer, from what the Bible says.

Jesus told his disciples to trust him because he was going to prepare a room for them in his 'Father's house', and then he would return to take them to be with him there for ever (John 14:1–3). But he told one of thieves crucified with him, 'Today you will be with me in paradise' (Luke 23:43).

Then again, Paul talks of the dead as those who have fallen asleep, who will be raised from death when Jesus comes again (1 Thessalonians 4:13–18). He writes elsewhere, though, 'I desire to depart and be with Christ, which is better by far' (Philippians 1:23), as if there will be no time lapse between dying and being with Christ.

These are mysteries with which we have to live, but I choose to believe that my deceased loved ones are now outside time and experiencing what G.K. Chesterton called 'the everlasting mercy' as well as the unimaginable, inconceivable 'things God has prepared for those who love him' (1 Corinthians 2:9).

Are you at peace about those you love who have died? Talk to God about this and allow his peace to fill you again.

JEAN WATSON

Getting real about emotions

Being in anguish, he prayed more earnestly, and his sweat was like drops of blood falling to the ground.

As I reread the Gethsemane stories (see also Matthew 26:36–45 and Mark 14:32–42), I am struck again by the emotions Jesus showed at this point in his life. The passages show us that he was sorrowful and troubled; he experienced feelings of weakness and exhaustion; he felt let down by his disciples and isolated; he was in emotional anguish; he was filled with fear and dread at what he was facing. Yet he prayed for and found the courage to stay the course.

Reading other stories of Jesus, I learn that he was sometimes tired and hungry, sad or joyful, disappointed or pleased, observant and compassionate, angry or amused and delighted. He felt real human emotions and was, I believe, honest about them.

How real are we about our emotions? We are all different temperamentally, so we feel things differently and express our feelings differently. What matters is whether we are real with ourselves about what we are feeling rather than being in denial, and whether the emotions we choose to show to others are genuine rather than put on for effect or as a cover-up.

For example, do we sometimes give the responses and show the emotions that we think we 'ought' to be showing as Christians? I have been told of a group of recently bereaved people who went about in celebratory mode because they felt they ought to be rejoicing that their loved one was with Jesus. Is this kind of behaviour honest about emotions? Does it follow the example that Jesus gave us?

Reflect on how real you are about your emotions and what this tells you about your or other people's 'ought's.

JEAN WATSON

Getting real about being rich or poor

'You say, "I am rich…" But you do not realise that you are wretched, pitiful, poor, blind and naked.'

Today's Bible passage tells us Jesus' words to the church in Laodicea. He calls them 'lukewarm' (v. 16) and says that although they think they are rich, in fact they are 'wretched, pitiful, poor, blind and naked'.

Jesus turns the world and its values upside down. Many of the first will be last and vice versa (Matthew 19:30); the hungry receive good things and the rich are sent away empty (Luke 1:53).

The church in Laodicea saw itself as rich, and, in the eyes of the world, it would have seemed so. The city was a banking centre and therefore wealthy; it manufactured clothes and carpets and had a medical school. There was nothing wrong with these achievements in and of themselves, but the fact that these were the Laodiceans' priorities, of which they were proud and in which they placed their trust, was what made the Christians spiritually poor. To be spiritually rich, they needed not the wealth that their banks provided but true 'gold'—the treasures that Jesus could give them. They needed to be clothed not in the garments they manufactured but in 'white clothes'—the goodness that Jesus could dress them in. They needed not the medicine that their medical school provided but 'eye salve'—Jesus' healing of their distorted vision and priorities.

When you have time, it is interesting to study Jesus' life and teaching and find out more about being 'rich towards God' (Luke 12:21). The Sermon on the Mount, for example (Matthew 5—7), commends the blessedness or spiritual richness of the meek, the merciful and peacemakers. It also highlights the importance of being reconciled rather than holding grudges and staying angry, self-discipline and faithfulness rather than self-indulgence, and overcoming evil with good rather than taking revenge.

Reflect thankfully on your true riches and bring to Jesus any 'poor' priorities or faulty spiritual eyesight.

JEAN WATSON

Making links

Ali Herbert writes:

We have spent the last fortnight looking at 'getting real' in a variety of areas in our lives. Jean Watson has guided us through the need to be authentic and genuine with each other and with ourselves in every area of our lives. Sometimes we need to take a second look at parts of our lives that we don't necessarily think of as 'spiritual', such as our personalities, our material lifestyles and our finances.

It seems to me that Miriam is a great example of someone in the Bible who was faced again and again with 'reality'—the reality of life under slavery, families torn apart, a desperate bid to escape and the struggles of life in harsh desert climes. She discovered that God was interested in rescuing his people and was a powerful God. He was full of goodness, yet jealous for his people's hearts—and the *truth* of the heart in particular. We see, too, that she continued to worship him.

This is quite a challenge to us as we go through both good and bad times. Will we choose to keep praising God or blame him for our circumstances instead? What will our attitudes be to the situations we find ourselves in? Will we choose to hold on to the hurt or let it go in his presence? To worship is definitely a choice.

Miriam may be one of those Bible characters that you've heard of (perhaps you know that she did a bit of dancing with a tambourine at one point) but have not studied very closely. However, she played a pivotal role in a major story of the Israelites in the Old Testament—the parting of the Red Sea and the escape from Egypt. We remember Moses as the key player in that event, but, as they say, behind every great man… (is a woman rolling her eyes!) If not for Miriam, there might have *been* no Moses, as she played the main role in rescuing him when he was a baby. She then stood by his side as he led the people through their years in the desert.

Miriam is a fascinating Bible character who seems very human to us in her strengths and weaknesses. This week, as Bola Adamolekun unpacks some of the history of this amazing woman, we will have the opportunity to learn from her life, her worship and even her mistakes.

Whose story?

The children of Amram were Aaron, Moses, and Miriam.

Genealogies can be fascinating. I love to jump on to a family history website and find out exactly how this person is related to that person. Perhaps this just reveals my nerdy tendencies, but I think it's more to do with my fascination with history and the fact that I love to read stories set in past times.

However, biblical genealogies tend to evoke the very opposite effect in me. My eyes glaze over and the only word I can remember by the end is 'begat'—not who did the begetting of whom. But these genealogies performed an important function for the people of the time. In the book of Numbers (for example, chs. 1 and 3), they showed how the land was to be divided and shared out among family groups and tribes. In 1 Chronicles 1—9, the lists of names enabled the Israelites to place themselves in their correct historical position, on their return from exile. They could link the generations back in time and say with confidence, 'I belong here.'

However, these genealogies were made up almost exclusively of the names of the sons—so why was Miriam included in a list of the sons of Levi? Indeed, who was Miriam to have been included with the famous pairing of Moses and Aaron in the significant history of the Israelites?

Imagine a mother crouching down to her daughters and sons to tell the story of Miriam, the sister of Moses and Aaron. Imagine their eyes widening at the tale of the basket in the river (Exodus 2:1–10) and the song of deliverance that Miriam sang (15:20–21), their puzzlement over the argument between Moses, Miriam and Aaron (Numbers 12:1–15) and their sorrow at learning where Miriam was buried (20:1).

The story they were told was of a flesh-and-blood person whom God used significantly within their history and who became part of God's story of salvation for all people.

Dear Lord Jesus, help me to see and remember all those events in our story that show I belong to you. Amen

BOLA ADAMOLEKUN

Nameless

For I brought you up from the land of Egypt, I redeemed you from the house of bondage; And I sent before you Moses, Aaron, and Miriam. O My people, remember now.

Some authors believe that unless a new character is going to feature prominently in their story, the character shouldn't be given a name. Clearly that bit of literary wisdom is not always employed in the Bible. For example, the two midwives in Exodus 1:15–19 are named, even though their parts in the story end in the same chapter. Yet when we meet Miriam for the first time, in Exodus 2:4, we can't even be sure it's her. In fact, of the three women who move that story ahead, none is named. All we know is that a mother, a sister and a daughter upset the plans of the ruling Pharaoh.

Our focus is on the sister who, in Exodus 2, watches over the baby Moses. Biblical tradition identifies her as Miriam, yet here in her introduction there is no indication that we will ever see her again. If this was a play at the theatre, we would see a young girl simply stepping on to the stage, delivering her lines and exiting. She is not introduced to us and, when she eventually returns to the stage, our attention is no longer on her. Her part is over—or is it?

Exodus 2 does not point forward to indicate that this unnamed character will one day be known as a leader of significance, but today's reading reveals a different viewpoint. In the epic story of God's saving relationship with Israel, Miriam is named as one of God's commissioned agents of salvation. Her story, by the end, has become far more significant than her unnamed beginning would suggest.

Often, we see our beginnings as a marker of who we are and who we might become. Instead, perhaps we can live our lives trusting that God can and will make much more of our lives than our beginnings, or even our ends, might suggest.

Dear Lord Jesus, here I am, choosing to be utterly surrendered to you with all of my past, present and future; in your name I pray. Amen

BOLA ADAMOLEKUN

Being and becoming

[Moses'] sister stood at a distance, to see what would happen to him.

I love reading stories of heroic characters overcoming the odds. It may be clichéd, but there is something to be said for a story about a lowly girl or boy who discovers that they are really the lost hope of a kingdom. I think these stories speak to us about significance and identity. What does it mean to be a significant person?

You could say that Miriam's story is of that type. She is introduced as one lowly girl, against the backdrop of a planned massacre of Israelite baby boys. Our protagonist is seen as just a girl in a culture that considers boys to be the potential change-makers, the threats to the ruling kingdom. As Miriam enters the story, she is a child without a name, without any power and of little threat to anyone.

Imagine being that child. The ruling government says that you are unimportant. You are no threat to their political power. There can be as many girls as possible and it will not matter to them. Neglected and ignored, how would you ever know yourself as significant in this time and this culture?

Exodus 2:4 states that this vulnerable girl stands at a distance and watches as her mother tries to save her baby brother. It is easy to read this 'watching from a distance' as a passive position, but the Hebrew words suggest something different. Our heroine can hardly hope to have any influence in this situation, yet she has deliberately taken a stand over it. She is not just watching, sidelined by the political powers and culture; she is watching and waiting for an opportunity that the only true God can provide.

Eternal Lord of time and space, of the very large and the very tiny, create in me a heart of hope for the things you want to change. Amen

BOLA ADAMOLEKUN

Who do you say you are?

Then his sister said to Pharaoh's daughter, 'Shall I go and get
you a nurse from the Hebrew women to nurse the child for you?'
Pharaoh's daughter said to her, 'Yes.' So the girl went and called
the child's mother.

As a child, reading heroic legends, I didn't mind whether the hero of
the story was a man or a woman. What mattered to me was the character of the person and the action they chose in response to the circumstances before them. I wanted to be like those characters—wise,
quick-thinking and ready to defend the weak and the young. I treasured
their simplicity, even their naivety.

The characters in Exodus 2 are neither simple nor naive. This is a
story of God's divine action in saving his people. He hears the cries
of their suffering and responds, sending a change-maker among them.
And who does he work with to bring about this change? A couple of
midwives, a young mother, a princess and a girl—hardly a roster of
heroic types. Yet this girl is quick to recognise an opportunity and uses
her 'powerless' appearance to aid God's divine opportunity. She tricks a
person in political power and offers an ingenious solution to a problem
that seemed hopeless.

Lest we forget how brave and quick-witted Miriam's actions were,
ask yourself, how did this young Hebrew slave girl dare to approach an
Egyptian princess and offer such wisdom? We often allow other people's definitions of us—who we are and what we are capable of—to
stand in the way of God's definition. In that moment when Miriam
made her approach to the princess, she stepped outside the world's
view of her and stood within God's view of her instead. As a result, she
was significantly used by God. It wasn't about her age, gender, appearance or physical ability; it was all about what God could achieve with
her availability.

---

*Who do people say you are? What do they say you are not? What does
God say in response? Listen to who God says you are, and remember,
this is your story with him.*

BOLA ADAMOLEKUN

Being human

While they were at Hazeroth, Miriam and Aaron spoke against Moses because of the Cushite woman whom he had married (for he had indeed married a Cushite woman); and they said, 'Has the Lord spoken only through Moses? Has he not spoken through us also?' And the Lord heard it.

Miriam has spoken out. She has Aaron by her side, but verse 1 gives her name before Aaron's, indicating that she is the leader in their complaint. She has accused Moses of marrying outside the tribe—again. His first wife, Zipporah, was a Midianite (Exodus 2:21; 3:1) and, although that could be excused by the fact that Moses was not living among his own people when he married her, this second, unnamed wife is also not an Israelite. You can almost hear Miriam fuming, 'Weren't there plenty of perfectly good Israelite women around?'

'Propriety' is described as the quality of appropriateness—doing what is fitting and in conformity with the norms and customs of the day. Sociologists have identified that women often act as the guardians of what is deemed proper and right, even in patriarchal societies. The women, more than the men, will ostracise a woman who, they believe, does not 'belong' in their midst.

Miriam is also challenging Moses in his role as a prophet. As the leading female prophet of her people, her complaint is both an accusation and a challenge to his authority.

At best, she has added to the growing list of complaints against Moses from the people—when, as his sister, she might have been expected to show loyalty. In addition, Miriam reveals herself to be prejudiced, a quality not appropriate in one who is a leader among her people.

There are far too many moments in my life when I wish I could take my words back. Whether or not it seemed a good idea at the time to speak out, the aftermath leaves me wishing I could hide—but that would mean I didn't take responsibility for my words. The alternative is not to stay silent but to love utterly and completely before I speak.

Dear Lord of all, reveal the hidden motives of my heart, of which I need to repent. Help me first to love those whom I need to challenge, and please help me to stay humble at all times. Amen

BOLA ADAMOLEKUN

Through the valley...

And Moses cried to the Lord, 'O God, please heal her.'

'It's unfair!' she cried out and then burst into tears. We hate unfairness: the feeling seems to be bred into us as children and we bristle with it as adults, particularly when we feel that justice is not being served.

Maybe even Miriam felt like this? When God withdraws, leaving behind the evidence of his judgement, she appears to have been the only one disciplined. How has Aaron got away with it? We're not told, but we do know that Aaron responds quickly when he sees that Miriam has been punished (v. 11). He acknowledges the wrongdoing and repents on behalf of himself and Miriam, choosing not to apportion blame but to look for a way forward. Aaron and, indeed, Moses intercede for her. She is instantly healed but the consequences of her actions remain with her for a while (v. 15).

We are told that God goes away and Miriam is banished from the camp for seven days. However, this same narrative also reveals that the words of banishment are also words about relationship: God is speaking of his relationship with Miriam as if it were between a father and daughter. His response is not a rejection of her or a vindictive punishment. He disciplines her but he also maintains lines of connection, announcing himself as her father in the midst of her fall.

It is important to remember that we will all make mistakes and that, when we do, God does not break his relationship with us or disown us. The consequence of Miriam's sin is a temporary banishment from her people. Even if our actions result in our being separated from all that we've held dear, God is still completely for us, completely willing to forgive and restore us.

Meditate on the words from Isaiah 53:5: 'By his stripes, we are healed'
(NKJV).

BOLA ADAMOLEKUN

Looking back, looking forward

Then the prophet Miriam, Aaron's sister, took a tambourine in her hand; and all the women went out after her with tambourines and with dancing.

I am not the best diary keeper but I do have a few journals from the early years of my journey with God. On occasion, I go back and read them, and sometimes I cry over how simple things seemed back then— how naive I was but also how joyful. The passing of time shades our experiences, adding texture, asking questions about who we thought we were and who we thought we would become.

I love to see how idealistic I was in the past, but I have also learned to treasure the questions I have now and the compassion they have taught me for those who are still struggling with their lives, their faith and their stories.

When I read of this exuberant Miriam, dancing, throwing a tambourine in the air, celebrating in the Lord's power and faithfulness, I think how simple life must have seemed then. God had delivered them from Egypt and things could only get better. Later on, as she entered the week of exile that we read about yesterday, did she remember her celebration and think what an ignominious end her story had had? How would she face returning to her community?

Let's pay attention to the little clues her story reveals. Numbers 20:1 tells us when and where Miriam died and was buried. She is counted as one of the heroes of Israel, alongside Moses and Aaron, in Micah 6:4 and 1 Chronicles 6:3. Details like these are written down for people accorded significance, not ignominy.

Our current situation, the mistakes we've made or the loss of our past enthusiasm can appear to be all-defining, but with God, there is so much more than we see. His faithfulness never depends on our abilities, our gifts, our successes or failures. He loves us and he is faithful. That is the defining significance to our stories.

Father, thank you that you love us, forgive us and restore us, and that all of this is your initiative. Help us to walk in your footsteps, loving others, forgiving them and seeking reconciliation. You are our story. Amen

BOLA ADAMOLEKUN

Don't forget to renew your subscription to *Day by Day with God*!

You might also like to consider a gift subscription for a friend.

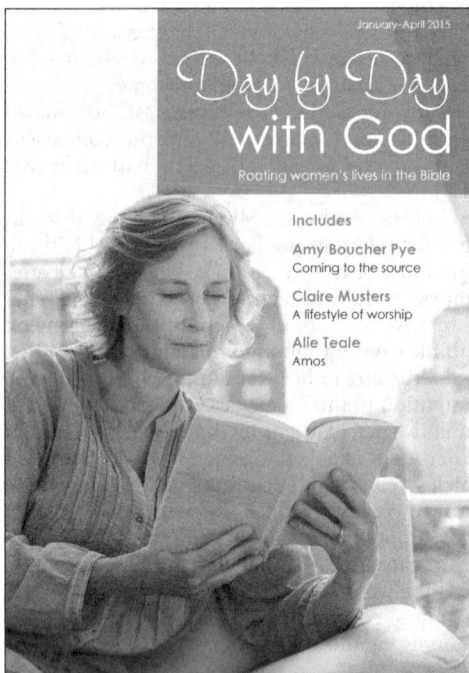

January–April 2015

Day by Day
with God

Rooting women's lives in the Bible

Includes

Amy Boucher Pye
Coming to the source

Claire Musters
A lifestyle of worship

Alie Teale
Amos

See page 144 for further information.

Making links

Amy Boucher Pye writes:

Water—it's the stuff of life. We're made of it and can't live without it. Although it can become stagnant and poisoned, fresh water brings renewal, cleansing and satisfaction. To those living in the developed world, it's always available at the flick of a wrist, but for those without easy access, the chore of gathering clean water for drinking, cooking and washing is time-consuming. I remember driving through Tanzania, awed by the strength of the women who were carrying large containers of it, often on their heads, for many kilometres. More recently, I've heard of friends whose pump broke in their home in Moldova. Getting fresh water from the nearby spring took several trips on a sledge through the snow. My friend said that when the pump was fixed, a hot bath had never felt so good.

I welcome you to these two weeks of thinking about living water—this common thing, created by God, which becomes powerful in his hands. Before writing these notes, I knew that water was special, but I began to discover deeper layers of meaning while engaging with stories from the Old and New Testaments. So we shall be reading about the water that existed before God created the world; the water of the Red Sea that parted for Moses during his miraculous escape from the Egyptians; the water from the heavens that comes down to earth, making it bud and grow, producing what God intends; the water that sprinkles us into new life; and, of course, Jesus, the source of living water for those who believe and trust in him.

See what I mean? Riches indeed! I'm excited to journey with you, and would love you to write to BRF with any revelations or pictures that God shows you during this fortnight about water and its properties.

This series culminates on Holy Saturday. As we reach the end of the season of Lent, it is fitting to think about the river of life in the city to come, which will bring nourishment and healing for the nations. As the Lord says, 'Come to the waters, all who are thirsty. Come and be refreshed.'

The stuff of life

In the beginning God created the heavens and the earth. Now the earth was formless and empty, darkness was over the surface of the deep, and the Spirit of God was hovering over the waters.

Have you ever noticed, in the Genesis 1 account, that *before* the six days of creation began, there was water? The earth was without form, but the Spirit of God was hovering over the waters. I hadn't seen that before, but I'm not surprised, for water is the stuff of life. More than half of our body is made of water and, if we go without, we'll only last about three days before dying of dehydration. We also perish spiritually if we don't drink from God's water of life.

God brings order out of chaos; he forms the waters into the expanses of heaven and earth, the sea and dry land. He then fills the oceans, lakes and rivers with life—a world below of creatures and plants and fish. The clouds rain down on the earth, bringing forth vegetation and providing water for the people made in God's image, and God sees that it is good.

This picture of creation in Genesis 1 comes, of course, before the fall of the world, before Adam and Eve disobey God and usher in sin, disease and pain. Water now can destroy—through flooding, overconsumption (water poisoning) and drowning. We have had to leave the perfect Eden.

Although water can refresh or drench, the Lord turns it into a living thing that will renew and cleanse. As we drink deeply, he quenches our thirst. As we wash our robes in his waters, we are cleaned. As we sit beside the still waters, we are refreshed.

Why not take a drink of water? As you do so, ask the Lord to reveal something about this common thing that you've never before realised or understood. How might God want to refresh you today through his living water, which existed before the creation of the world?

Lord God, Creator of the heavens and the earth, expand my understanding of and love for you and your creation. Amen

AMY BOUCHER PYE

Walls of water

The Lord said to Moses, '... Raise your staff and stretch out your hand over the sea to divide the water so that the Israelites can go through the sea on dry ground. I will harden the hearts of the Egyptians so that they will go in after them. And I will gain glory.'

Water is God's servant, as we see when Moses parts the Red Sea so that the Israelites can escape the Egyptians. You probably know the story: the Israelites were slaves in Egypt, serving Pharaoh for years without freedom. Moses was the timid instrument whom God used to lead his people out of bondage—Moses, who was so scared to speak that he even employed his brother as his mouthpiece. God revealed his power and strength again and again as the Israelites tried to secure their freedom, through sending horrific plagues of hail, gnats and even death. Moses' confidence grew as he witnessed the acts of the Lord.

However, the Israelites seem to need yet another amazing miracle to convince them that God truly is releasing them into the land of milk and honey. As they leave Egypt, Pharaoh changes his mind and sends his best armies after them. God instructs Moses and the people to camp near the Red Sea. Grumbles and fear erupt from the Israelites as they see the Egyptians bearing down on them, but Moses obeys the Lord and the unthinkable occurs: as Moses stretches out his hand, the waters part, forming a wall of water on the left and a wall of water on the right. Through the middle is not even mud, but dry ground.

Are we like the Israelites, murmuring against the Lord and blind to his miracles in our lives? Do we believe that he can part the waters we face? Or do we exist in a state of disappointment and discouragement, not believing that God will work his wonders for us? Today, ask the Lord to open your eyes to God's hand in things big or small. Request from him the faith to see him parting the sea.

Lord of Moses, may you take our stammers and our small attempts to speak your word and multiply them for your kingdom and your glory. Strike our hearts with faith. Amen

AMY BOUCHER PYE

Water from the rock

The Lord answered Moses, '… Take in your hand the staff with which you struck the Nile, and go. I will stand there before you by the rock at Horeb. Strike the rock, and water will come out of it for the people to drink.'

Although the Israelites have experienced God's miracles, still they grumble against him. They may have seen their attackers drowning in the Red Sea as the waters merged together, but they don't believe that the Lord will provide for their daily needs. At Marah, where the water is bitter, they cry out in desperation. The Lord answers, showing Moses a piece of wood with which he can make the water sweet. Then, in the Desert of Sin (aptly named), the Israelites complain against Moses and the Lord: 'We're hungry!' The Lord meets their needs with manna and quails, but the lesson doesn't stick. As we see in today's passage, again they become furious with Moses when they grow thirsty. Moses even fears for his life, thinking they will stone him. I wonder if the Lord gets tired of all of their complaining—yet he rescues them again.

The miracle we read about here is seemingly unthinkable: water from a rock? But both are created by God and are under his direction. What might seem beyond the realm of possibility is simple for the Lord. Can we grasp this?

A friend of mine is suffering through a family situation in which she is tempted to see no hope. Brother is pitted against sister and the dying aunt is angry with them all. Words are unleashed that wound; bitterness reigns and hurt multiplies. This is her rock to offer up to the Lord: what staff should she strike it with? Can he somehow bring his living, refreshing water to flow out of it?

Humanly, we look at the facts of a situation and despair, but, as we stand on the promises of God, we see him moving and working. I pray that his living water will flush out the impurities in my friend's family, bringing health, peace and joy.

Lord God, I'm facing some huge boulders that seem dry and dead. Show me how I can strike them so that you can bring living water out of them. Amen

AMY BOUCHER PYE

Healing rain

Then the fire of the Lord fell and burned up the sacrifice, the wood, the stones and the soil, and also licked up the water in the trench. When all the people saw this, they fell prostrate and cried, 'The Lord—he is God! The Lord—he is God!'

'The troubler of Israel': this is how King Ahab describes the prophet Elijah when Elijah warns Ahab that his people will suffer a long drought because they've turned their backs on God (v. 17). Three dry years later, Elijah invites Ahab to a standoff. Who is the true God—Yahweh or the gods of Baal and Asherah?

I love this story of Elijah facing nearly 1000 false prophets. While they work themselves up into a frenzy, frenetically calling on their gods and even drawing their own blood, Elijah sits in peace, watching the spectacle. He knows that his God is the only true God, and his God will show up.

Although the period of drought has made water scarce, Elijah douses the sacrifice not once, not twice, but three times—so much that water overflows the trench around the altar. He calls on the Lord and the Lord responds. Fire eats up the sacrifice and licks up every last drop of water.

Then Elijah waits for the clouds of rain, for he knows that the Lord will send them. He's not disappointed: soon the healing rains come. The Lord has used the drought to bring about repentance and to prove that he is God.

We don't often think about God controlling the elements as a means of discipline. Do you think he still does? I hope not. I hope that Jesus' sacrificial death will have brought a measure of healing to the earth, but I know too that the effects of sin and selfishness result in miseries to our earth. We can pray that God, in his mercy, would stem the rain when the earth is soaked, calm the tremors of the molten crust and bring healing moisture during periods of drought.

How can you pray for the earth's healing?

Creator Lord, forgive us for misusing the gifts you have bestowed on us. Open our eyes to ways in which we can take better care of our environment. Amen

AMY BOUCHER PYE

Water of life

Elisha sent a messenger to say to [Naaman], 'Go, wash yourself seven times in the Jordan, and your flesh will be restored and you will be cleansed.'

A great and important man almost misses a blessing from God because he doesn't want to humble himself and follow instructions. Naaman, a commander in a non-Israelite army, thinks he can direct the prophet Elisha to bring about his own healing, but the prophet follows a higher authority—the true and living God. Naaman isn't in the driving seat. Only his servants are wise enough to encourage him to do what the prophet says—namely, wash seven times in the River Jordan. When he humbles himself, gone is his leprosy.

Water plays a key role in this story as God's agent for effecting his healing. Naaman has to die to his old self, his desire to do things his way, and submit to God's ways. When he washes himself according to Elisha's specific instructions, he is healed and, more importantly, he embraces new life. He sheds his old self with his demands and personal requirements and realises that God is the source of healing. The God of Elisha is the one who brings new life, symbolised by the waters of baptism.

Elisha's refusal of payment reinforces the old self/new self paradigm shift. Naaman expects to pay for his healing, but Elisha shows him that it's the gift of God. Thus, when Elisha's crooked servant Gehazi extracts some silver and clothing from Naaman, he is punished. His sin is revealed as the greedy hoarding that it is.

Water is cleansing. Why not take some time today to wash yourself, perhaps soaking in a bath, revelling in a hot shower or holding your hands under the tap? As you do so, picture the Lord freeing you of bitterness, pain or lack of belief while you receive his love, grace and hope. Embrace the new life God has given you.

Father, help us to shed our old self and to be made new in the attitudes of our minds, putting on the new self; created like you in true righteousness and holiness. Amen (Based on Ephesians 4:22–24)

AMY BOUCHER PYE

The good shepherd

The Lord is my shepherd, I lack nothing. He makes me lie down in green pastures, he leads me beside quiet waters, he refreshes my soul.

Still waters running deep: this was the picture that a woman had for me when I was leading a prayer retreat, and it touched me to the core. She didn't know me well, which made the image even more precious. The Lord seemed to be saying that I was rooted in him, that his living water was filling me and drawing me into his depths of wisdom and love.

All those born of the Spirit have access to the same waters of life. In this most popular psalm, King David speaks of the Lord leading him to quiet waters and refreshing his soul. In David's setting, of course, green pastures and streams of water were rare. Much more common was dry, dusty, rocky terrain, where shepherds would have had to walk miles in search of a verdant oasis.

This psalm is so well loved because it communicates truth and wisdom in succinct yet poetic words. The table the Lord invites us to (v. 5) could be the table of Holy Communion, where we eat the food set out for us by the Lord Jesus. The quiet waters could be the waters of baptism, in which we are immersed, cleansed and made members of a new community. Although we face trials, the good shepherd will never leave or forsake us.

A faith-building exercise is to take this psalm and personalise it. One way is to replace the word 'shepherd' with the role of a boss or superior. A writer could say, 'The Lord is my publisher'; an actor, 'The Lord is my director'; an insurance broker, 'The Lord is my CEO'; or a teacher, 'The Lord is my head teacher'. Consider rewriting the psalm along these lines today and see how the Lord blesses you.

Lord God, shepherd of our souls, lead us to the deep and quiet waters today, that we might drink and be satisfied. Amen

AMY BOUCHER PYE

Directing our souls

As the deer pants for streams of water, so my soul pants for you, my God. My soul thirsts for God, for the living God.

Often in the Christian life, we have times not only of drenching but also of drought. When we first turn to Christ, we might experience a period of joy and heightened emotion: we feel alive and close to God, seeing his hand in all manner of ways. But as we journey along, we will face times when we feel as if we're living in a desert, without water and without hope. The Lord seems far from us; when we cry out to him, we sense only silence.

The psalmist here is thinking back to the times of rich communion with God; he yearns for the Lord as a deer pants for water in a dry and weary land. He fears that the torrent of emotions within him will overcome him, as if he's submerged in the waterfall's roar or swept under the power of the waves.

Yet he knows that deep calls to deep and the Lord is with him, even if his soul is downcast and he doesn't feel God's presence. In writing the psalm, he is reminding his soul—his inner being—of the ways in which the Lord has loved him. He is educating his soul to continue to hope in the Lord.

When we are in a period of drought and are tempted to believe that God has left us, we need to direct our souls to God's ways and truth. Our memories might be filled with times of rejoicing—the 'shouts of joy and praise' that the psalmist remembers in verse 4—but we think we'll never again feel this joy. With the psalmist, then, we need to tell ourselves, our soul, to keep hoping in the Lord, for he will lead us beside those quiet waters. He will rescue us, restore us and renew us.

Consider how you've been created—body, mind, spirit, soul. How do the various parts fit together? Do you find this idea humbling or empowering? (Search online for Dallas Willard's teaching on the soul.)

AMY BOUCHER PYE

Flourish

As the rain and the snow come down from heaven… so that it yields seed for the sower and bread for the eater, so is my word that goes out from my mouth: it will not return to me empty, but will accomplish what I desire.

Isaiah 55 has long been one of my favourite chapters in the Bible. In fact, my husband and I had it read at our wedding, for we wanted our lives to reflect the upside-down kingdom of God, where we could invite people to eat without cost and not labour in vain. More recently, verse 10 (quoted above) was the passage of scripture that I felt the Lord highlighted for me for the year. I especially focused on one word: 'flourish'.

God's word accomplishes what he intends. His water flows to the earth through rain and snow, bringing life and refreshment and nourishment. The seeds bud and grow, turning into living organisms, including wheat for bread. The bread of life (Jesus) meets all of our needs, satisfying our hunger.

When I look back over the year, though, considering my word 'flourish', I am tempted to disbelieve God. The deepest hope I was harbouring was to secure a US publisher for the book I'm writing, and that came to naught. Flourish? Harrumph. But in reaching these conclusions, I was seeing the year through my lens, not God's (and missing the point of the preceding verse, which says that his ways are higher than mine). When I asked God to show me the year from his point of view, I soon recognised many areas of flourishing—my publishing and (other) writing work, my discipling friendships at church, my speaking engagements on biblical topics, the enriching travel we enjoyed, my relationship with my husband and children. Why ignore all of that goodness?

As I look through the list, I reorientate my mind and my emotions, grateful for God's mercy and love, thankful that he does send his word in season and that it plants and takes root and grows into a wonderful creation all its own. How is God's word making you flourish?

Lord God, please show us your perspective when we are tempted to interpret our life events according to our own lens. Give us your eyes to see your eternal perspective. Amen

AMY BOUCHER PYE

Droughts and drenchings

The Lord will guide you always; he will satisfy your needs in a sun-scorched land and will strengthen your frame. You will be like a well-watered garden, like a spring whose waters never fail.

I've been introduced to the wonders of Spain through leading retreats at a restful and stretching place there (El Palmeral). The Mediterranean sun warms my bones, which have grown cold in a draughty Victorian English vicarage. The starkly different flora and fauna jolt my senses. The flavours of the Spanish cooking delight my taste buds and the space for time with God fills up my thirsty places.

But I've only just learned about a tradition of flood irrigation that is common there, introduced by the Moors from Arabic lands. After seasons of complete dryness, the Spanish release water in channels when the ground needs drenching. This cycle of drought and drenching, drought and drenching, echoes that of God's seasons of planting, growth, pruning, sowing, reaping, death and so on (and resonates with our Bible passage on Saturday).

In Isaiah's prophecy, the Lord rejects the false fasts of his people—those days given to fasting in name, which are marked by quarrels, self-interested actions and strife. Only when they humble themselves and call on the Lord will he answer their needs. Will he satisfy their droughts with the drenching of his living water? Will he enclose their garden with protective walls to keep the never-failing springs safe?

Have you considered what sort of season you're living in? Is the sun shining on you and your loved ones, so that you revel in God's blessings and delight, or does it feel like a time of enforced rest or early retirement? If we keep in mind God's ecosystem, we'll more readily remember that though we may weep at night, joy will come in the morning (Psalm 30:5, acknowledging that the Lord's sense of timing differs from our own). Join me in giving thanks for the lessons we're learning, whatever season we're in.

Lord, you are the master gardener. You prune us, that we might bear more fruit. You graft us into yourself, the true and living vine. May we look to you for our joy this day. Amen

AMY BOUCHER PYE

New heart

'I will sprinkle clean water on you, and you will be clean; I will cleanse you from all your impurities… I will give you a new heart and put a new spirit in you; I will remove from you your heart of stone and give you a heart of flesh.'

The people of Israel had messed up again. They had left the ways of God and instead pursued their own desires and own gods. Time after time, the Lord had come back to redeem them, and here the prophet Ezekiel promises that God will again save. This time, though, he's doing it for the sake of his name, for his holiness (v. 22). He decides to change the Israelites from the inside out, so that they can worship him in purity.

Tinkering with minor concerns won't be sufficient. What is needed is a complete overhaul in his people—removal of their hearts of stone and replacement with hearts of flesh. Then they will follow his decrees and keep his commands; then they can live in the land he bequeathed to their ancestors. Then they can be his people. What would be the outward sign of all this inward work? The sprinkling of water—God's living water, his created matter that acts as an outward symbol of an inward change.

A couple of years ago, I attended the baptism of a young woman whose father had died when she was eight. Although her earthly father had abandoned her (not willingly, but through disease), her heavenly Father had not. Witnessing her being submerged in the pool and emerging as a new creation moved me. The prayers of her parents were fulfilled on that day, the water symbolising the work God was doing in her life: he had promised that he would not abandon her as an orphan.

Have you been baptised? If so, ask the Lord to show you how that outer symbol has effected change in your life. If not, ask the Lord if a public act of commitment like this is something you should pursue. We all can ask the Lord to melt our hearts of stone and give us his hearts of flesh.

Make mine a heart of flesh, Lord, that I may feel deeply, love devotedly and live in hope. Amen

AMY BOUCHER PYE

The well of life

Jesus answered, 'Everyone who drinks this water will be thirsty again, but whoever drinks the water I give them will never thirst. Indeed, the water I give them will become in them a spring of water welling up to eternal life.'

Jesus wasn't afraid to break the conventions of his day. A Jewish rabbi would never, because of issues of gender and race, talk with the Samaritan woman who was drawing water from a well during the heat of the day. She, a social outcast, probably held her head low in shame, trying to avoid the stares and the condescension of those who saw her as a 'loose' woman, but here she meets Jesus, the man who can forgive and make her new.

They are at the well of his ancestors—Jacob's well, where Jacob first met Rachel. In a meeting that will similarly change lives, Jesus turns to the one called 'Shameful' and sees her for who she really is, 'Beloved'. He engages her in a conversation, in which she starts off sassy and perhaps sarcastic. But when he reveals her vulnerabilities—her connection with many men—she cracks open her heart with rejoicing that, finally, here is a man who truly knows her.

Water is a key part of the story. Jesus humbles himself, asking her to serve him, and then reveals that he is the source of the water that truly satisfies. As the unnamed woman receives this water, she is cleansed and made new. She who, minutes before, was avoiding her fellow villagers now runs to share the good news.

No matter what our sin—sexual impurity, gossip, pride or hardheartedness—Jesus invites us to drink of his living water and to sink our bucket into his well, so that we might share water with a people and a land that are thirsty, needing to be slaked. His water gives relief and builds up and, even as we offer it to others, we can't help being cleansed and renewed ourselves.

Father God, thank you for the water that cleanses, refreshes and satisfies our thirst. Show me someone with whom I can share your water today. Amen

AMY BOUCHER PYE

Come to the waters

On the last and greatest day of the festival, Jesus stood and said in a loud voice, 'Let anyone who is thirsty come to me and drink. Whoever believes in me, as Scripture has said, rivers of living water will flow from within them.'

Jesus arrives in Jerusalem during the Jewish Feast of Tabernacles, in the final autumn of his life. This feast was the third in the agricultural cycle, celebrating the autumn harvest. It also incorporated prayers for rain, as the land would then be affected by drought.

Opposition to Jesus was growing, but he didn't shy away from proclaiming who he was. On the final day of the feast, during the climax of the water ceremony, Jesus made the stunning pronouncement that he is the source of living water; if people will come and drink, then streams of living water will flow from within them. Those hearing him were divided in their response. Some thought he might be the Messiah, but others wanted to seize and kill him. Probably, they believed he was being blasphemous by linking himself to Yahweh, for the prophet Jeremiah had called the Lord the spring of living water (Jeremiah 2:13; 17:13).

When I think about living water flowing from within, I see a rushing stream with crystal-clear water that brings life to all it touches. As the water moves, it shapes and smooths the rocks underneath and it flushes out any murky residue.

Jesus is the source of living water and, as he lives in us through his Spirit, he will provide healing for our hurts and will oil the relational wheels with our loved ones. He will enable us to give a gracious reply even when we are spent, and will provide a life-giving solution when we are searching for wisdom. His living water in us will leave us cleansed, refreshed and fortified as we engage with the people around us. As the rivers flow from within us, we too can take others to this life-giving water.

'Let those who are thirsty come; and let all who wish take the free gift of the water of life' (Revelation 22:17).

AMY BOUCHER PYE

Be baptised

Peter replied, 'Repent and be baptised, every one of you, in the name of Jesus Christ for the forgiveness of your sins. And you will receive the gift of the Holy Spirit.'

It is fitting that we consider this testimony of Peter today, Good Friday. If you have time, read the whole of Acts 2, taking in Peter's succinct summary of the fulfilment of Joel's prophecy—how Jesus was killed according to God's plan and how, risen from the dead, he poured out the Holy Spirit on Pentecost.

What a picture of God's upside-down kingdom! Although Jesus was killed, yet he offers his murderers freedom and life. As theologian David Gooding says, 'They had crucified the second person of the Trinity; he was offering them the third' (*True to the Faith*, Gospel Folio, p. 55). All the people needed to do was repent and be baptised; they would then receive the empowering Holy Spirit.

Shelves of books have been published on baptism. Is it for adults or children? Is it necessary for salvation? What I think we should consider today is that it's an outward symbol of an inward reality. After Peter called people to repent, 3000 responded and stood publicly to be baptised. They received the new life of the Spirit.

I had the privilege of sponsoring a friend when she was baptised a few years ago. Because our church didn't have a source of hot water that would reach the baptismal pool, our vicar baptised by affusion: he poured three buckets of (warm) water over the heads of those being baptised. My friend said the water was so powerful that at one point she thought she was drowning; afterwards she realised that this physical sensation was not only due to the strong force of the water, but also because her old self was dying as she received her new self in Christ.

May we receive a fresh infilling of the Holy Spirit as we consider the death of our Lord.

Lord Jesus Christ, you gave all of yourself that I might live. May I be cleansed and renewed, that I might share your good news with others. Amen

AMY BOUCHER PYE

Water without cost

He said to me: 'It is done. I am the Alpha and the Omega, the Beginning and the End. To the thirsty I will give water without cost from the spring of the water of life.'

Today is Holy Saturday, a day of waiting for the fulfilment of the promises of God—that he who witnessed his Son dying a horrific death will raise him to life, thereby bestowing forgiveness and salvation to his children.

Although we wait, we know how the story ends—but we haven't yet welcomed the new heavens and new earth that the apostle John writes of in Revelation. We long to enjoy the never-ending presence of God, where there will be no more night, death, mourning or pain, where we will drink without cost from the spring of the water of life.

The father of a dear friend died recently, just six months after being diagnosed with cancer. My friend and her husband had moved close to her parents, planning to share their lives and ministry for the decades they hoped remained. As it became clear that the father would succumb to this disease, he continued to live with integrity and faith. He created memories for his children and grandchildren, writing them letters that they will treasure for ever. He enjoyed his last Christmas with his family, singing carols and watching the kids open presents with delight, and when he died, on the last day of the year, he did so 'in his own bed in the quiet of his own home with his own family and the thick presence of his own God' (from the sermon preached by his son-in-law).

This man of God now enjoys the new life in his resurrection body. He stands in the holy city, revelling in its brilliance and splendour. His robes are washed clean; he has walked through the gates and taken residence in the city; he has claimed the free gift of the water of life, life-giving water. Come, Lord Jesus.

Triune God, send to us your living water. Wash us clean, sustain us, refresh us, renew us—for your glory. Amen

AMY BOUCHER PYE

Making links

Chris Leonard writes:

I've had a horrible two years—not all bad, and not as bad as for many others of my acquaintance, nor as bad as what King David went through. Yet two deaths and several major operations, plus physical and emotional pain in the family, have made the time unpleasant enough to understand some of the 'pits' that David wrote of 3000 years ago. I've found his psalms helpful, not least because they, like me and these notes, go on a rollercoaster journey. God rescues us from one pit of despair; then, either through our own fault or through circumstances beyond our control, we're plunged into another. Sometimes God is with us in the pit; at others he seems to disappear, leaving us wallowing.

It's so easy to spiral down the plughole of 'poor me', especially when people keep saying, 'Oh dear, you've had one thing after another—poor you!' But self-pity doesn't help. I read of David, in far worse adversity than mine, instructing his soul, his eyes or his voice to be lifted up to the Lord. He thanked God for his rescues and blessings in the past and praised his goodness, power, love and righteousness. That's how he began to trust God wholeheartedly again. His circumstances might not have changed but his perspective on them did. I tried that and it works—but not always.

Eventually, I found that the light I saw when emerging from the latest pit served merely to dazzle and confuse me before I plunged into the next one. Worry became a habit. I wasn't sleeping and found myself teetering on the edge of something very dark and scary—call it burnout. I had kept going, as one does. When I had to give things up, I felt an all-round failure. Yet, when I came to write these notes, I found many more references to God lifting us than to our lifting his name or lifting our souls to him. He doesn't rely on us pulling ourselves up by our own bootstraps—even helpful spiritual ones. David knew that, when we are most poor and needy, even though we sometimes have to wait for rescue, God himself lifts us. I've certainly found those promises to be true.

That brings us in timely fashion to the ultimate lifting-up of Easter—to all that Christ's resurrection means for us, which David never knew but we can.

Resurrection!

'When David had served God's purpose in his own generation...
he was buried with his ancestors and his body decayed. But
the one whom God raised from the dead did not see decay...
Through him everyone who believes is set free from every sin.'

Happy Easter! And welcome, after the grief of Friday and yesterday, to
the ultimate lifting, the ultimate hopeful good news. As Paul says in
1 Corinthians 15:14 and 22, without Christ's resurrection our faith
would be useless, but because he was raised, we are made alive in him.

Celebrating Easter in France, I found that the word for 'Resurrected
One' is 'Ressuscité'. In English, though, 'resuscitation' is too weak a
word, meaning only 'revival from unconsciousness' rather than 'raising
from death'. In today's Bible verses, Paul is talking about the amazing
truth of resurrection that we see in Jesus.

In a sense, God saved David from death several times, enabling him
to continue the fullest of lives. In Psalm 16:8–11, David says, 'I keep
my eyes always on the Lord. With him at my right hand, I shall not be
shaken. Therefore my heart is glad and my tongue rejoices; my body
also will rest secure, because you will not abandon me to the realm of
the dead, nor will you let your faithful one see decay. You make known
to me the path of life; you will fill me with joy in your presence, with
eternal pleasures at your right hand.' Hallelujah! Those words are even
more true of Jesus.

David did die eventually, but more was to come. Jesus needed to be
'lifted up' on the cross to draw all people to himself (John 12:32). Then
came the resurrection: he was raised to the right hand of the Father in
glory, defeating death as the wages of sin, restoring our relationship
with God, and raising us with him. Even though we and our loved ones
'taste death', we won't stay in death. Let's rejoice as we glimpse our
destination!

_____

*Pray through and meditate on Ephesians 1:17–23, verses that reveal
more of the riches of what Jesus' resurrection means for us here on earth.*
                                                    CHRIS LEONARD

The humble lifted high

You save the humble but bring low those whose eyes are haughty... With your help I can advance against a troop; with my God I can scale a wall... He makes my feet like the feet of a deer; he causes me to stand on the heights.

It's uplifting to praise God and acknowledge all that he has done. Here David celebrates how God has lifted him. Remember, this insignificant younger brother from out-of-the-way Bethlehem, who was anointed king while still a shepherd boy, killed the enemy giant Goliath through his faith in a powerful God plus one small stone. He waited years to rule, depending on God while the current king tried to kill him. Once he was reigning, David drove powerful enemy tribes from the land so that the tribes of Israel could live there peacefully. Declared 'a man after God's heart' (1 Samuel 13:14), he was entrusted with fulfilling God's purposes.

God did indeed lift this humble man high, yet I've struggled with David's easy-sounding assertions, such as 'With my God I can scale a wall', as well as Paul's claim, 'I can do all things through him who strengthens me' (Philippians 4:13, NRSV). I've had to grasp that God does not magically transform us into Olympic pole-vaulters or weight-lifters. In 2 Samuel 22, we find David singing the triumphant words of Psalm 18 immediately before his last words, at the end of all the ups and downs of his life. The biblical giants of faith all experienced difficulties and struggles.

Psalm 18 exults in the crushing of enemies as God fought for David. Being short of human enemies, I used to find such thoughts difficult until I realised that my enemies are internal—a lack of trust in God, selfishness and worry. He can help me fight those attitudes. I still question David's suggestion that God helped him because he was righteous (vv. 20–24), as we know that he too had sinned and needed forgiveness. Perhaps he meant that he had fallen, sorted it out with God and been lifted up again.

Thank God, humbly, for lifting you—or you could pray Psalm 61:2–3 instead: 'I call as my heart grows faint... For you have been my refuge, a strong tower against the foe.'

CHRIS LEONARD

Sin lifted

Let the bones you have crushed rejoice... Create in me a pure heart, O God, and renew a steadfast spirit within me. Do not cast me from your presence or take your Holy Spirit from me. Restore to me the joy of your salvation.

Psalm 51 records how David prayed after his own conscience failed so catastrophically that the prophet Nathan had to tell him that causing a man's death to cover up your adultery with his wife is not acceptable to God! We're all blind to our own sins sometimes, but David's massive blind spots show how power can corrupt even godly people and once-good rulers. If pride comes before a fall, the powerful fall the farthest. How we need to pray for our rulers and church leaders!

In terms of eternity, 'the wages of sin is death' (Romans 6:23), but sin may carry heavy consequences in this life too. Trust, once broken, is hard to restore. Sin weighs us down emotionally and spiritually even when we don't acknowledge our guilt. A massive effort is required to live in denial, and banishing God's presence from our lives causes us huge pain. Before God lifted those weights and cleansed him, David needed to acknowledge that God was right and he was wrong, and choose to follow God's way.

Some people who are brought up in Christian homes reject faith later because 'it just makes you feel guilty'. I hope that church teaching hasn't led them astray, because the opposite is true. We are all guilty— but Christian faith doesn't leave us stuck there. Even 1000 years before Christ came to save us from our sins, David didn't stay bowed under guilt and shame's destructive power. He was certain that God, far from despising 'a broken and contrite heart' (v. 17), would restore the joy of his salvation. Although he had become more aware of his own weaknesses and temptations, David didn't despair; rather, he trusted that the restored presence of the Holy Spirit would keep him on the right path. Praise God that he restores us faithfully from all our sin, failures and brokenness.

'Blessed is the one whose transgressions are forgiven, whose sins are covered' (Psalm 32:1). Meditate on Psalm 51, 32 or 139 as you ask God to search your heart and keep you walking in his ways.

CHRIS LEONARD

Lifting our whole selves Godwards

You, Lord, are forgiving and good, abounding in love to all who call to you... Teach me your way, Lord, that I may rely on your faithfulness; give me an undivided heart, that I may fear your name.

Here David is 'poor and needy' (v. 1), begging for God's help—and the psalm describes no dramatic rescue. However, David had been trusting in his powerful fear that arrogant, ruthless and godless men would succeed in taking his life. Then, after lifting his soul to God and remembering that God's love once delivered him even from the depths of the grave, he transferred his trust to the divine compassion, faithfulness and comfort. Maybe that was the answer to his prayer that God would give him an 'undivided heart' to fear God's name (v. 11). God's name is love. Perfect love banishes fear. If we redirect all our focus and all our fears to him, peace reigns.

Perhaps it's like travelling by hot-air balloon. I've not tried it (I'm too nervous) but I know I wouldn't get far by standing on the ground, watching longingly, or even by stepping in with one foot. We need our undivided selves to jump right in and relinquish control of our lives to the one who is skilled in flying through capricious winds.

Do we really trust God or do we trust insurance policies, pension provision, ourselves, our allies or the state? It's usually irresponsible not to make some sensible provision for the future, of course, but how we need his wisdom to walk in his ways and truth in these difficult matters! During our family's health crises, I saw a lack of compassionate provision for the sick, especially the elderly and dying. I started to fear for my own generation, worrying that if things are so bad for older people now, they will be worse by the time we reach that stage! I lost my trust that heaven would help; fear and confusion ruled, not God. But he heard my cries, sending an unexpected, vivid 'picture' of my mother, safe on a ledge part way down a precipice, reassuring me that the nursing home she'd just entered was his perfect provision before he called her home.

Lord, how often we let ourselves be robbed by external circumstances of the peace and joy you have given us. Help us board your 'balloon' with our heart and trust undivided—and soar where you want us to go.

CHRIS LEONARD

Lifting the broken

Blessed are those who dwell in your house; they are ever praising you. Blessed are those whose strength is in you, whose hearts are set on pilgrimage. As they pass through the Valley of Baka, they make it a place of springs... They go from strength to strength.

'Baka' means 'weeping'. I'm good at that—but, if caught in public, I used to flee, embarrassed. Now I go with it, finding that way less bitter and more restorative.

Imagine people sweating their way through Israel's semi-desert, with its bandit-filled ravines, and suddenly finding an oasis! Does God sometimes transform our suffering, our 'valleys of weeping', into refreshing places that lift others up? That was certainly the case for Jesus—and for amazing people like Nelson Mandela. I know that the best comforters are those who have wept themselves.

Here, David is the thirsty one—thirsty for God. 'Come, all you who are thirsty, come to the waters,' says Isaiah 55:1. Sometimes finding the way to 'dwell in [God's] house' involves a difficult pilgrimage, during which we need refreshment. Everyone who lives with stress needs rest—not the passive, TV-watching kind, but the true rest in God's restoring presence that was the intention behind his provision of the sabbath.

During my recent troubles, I found it extremely difficult to enter an awareness of his presence. The constant churning of my worried thoughts blocked the way. I tried, each morning, at least to thank him for the new day, to ask for the particular gifts, strengths and compassion needed to face its daunting challenges, and to reassert my desire to be with and walk with him. I read the Psalms and continued going to Sunday worship, even though being there made me weep buckets sometimes. Simply seeing faithful servants of God lifted me. Their words and actions of love touched me, and the worship itself, the eternal truths, quenched my thirst a little, so that sometimes I could rest in Jesus' love and find some restoration for my soul.

Lord, thank you that you lift the broken and strengthen those who know they are weak. Thank you that the thirsty, hurting ones find you, and thank you for your acceptance, your restorative rest.

CHRIS LEONARD

Lifting heavy responsibility

When anxiety was great within me, your consolation brought me joy.

A man in our church works roughly half the year for the UN in Afghanistan. Convinced that God has called him there and will protect him, he appears never to have an anxious thought, despite the horrendous living and working conditions and all the dangers. I admire him but I couldn't be like him in a million years.

Comforted to find a psalmist who experienced great anxiety, I sought clues here to how God consoled him. This psalm is not attributed to David but is clearly written by someone who is upright, with a degree of responsibility, who hates the wickedness he sees but lacks the power base to do anything about it. That sounds like a classic cause of stress. It reminds me of Christians I know today who struggle to do right within huge organisations, only to find themselves under attack or even dismissed, with the good they have achieved reversed.

The psalmist lifts up the situation honestly to God, putting his faith in one who will act justly. He acknowledges God's help and finds refuge in him. I guess he's saying, 'I can't do this, God—but you can, so over to you!'

My sense of helplessness concerning my responsibilities for ailing elderly parents wasn't caused by corruption, but the responsibility wore me down, building into a state of anxiety over those two difficult years. I'd hand everything to God, then grab it back. I'd ask, 'How long?' Yet, with hindsight, I can see that God did make amazing provision—through church friends of both our mothers, who lived nearby and gave their time and compassion unstintingly; through my mum's wonderful nursing home; and through our son and his young wife who moved in with my mum-in-law, caring for her in the last 18 months of her life and enabling her to die at home, as she wished.

Lord, you do hear, you see, you teach us if we will trust you and listen, and you do rescue and defend us. Thank you for the times when your consolation even brings joy to our souls.

CHRIS LEONARD

Lifted from pit to song

He lifted me out of the slimy pit, out of the mud and mire; he set my feet on a rock and gave me a firm place to stand. He put a new song in my mouth, a hymn of praise to our God.

After various medical emergencies and long hospital stays, my mum-in-law died in June 2012. Meanwhile, our daughter-in-law, who had been looking after her at home, awaited the removal of agonising gallstones. That October, my mother was taken by ambulance to hospital and did not return home before she died in January 2013. In May, while we were still processing all of this, we were about to take Dad away for a break when our daughter-in-law, now minus gallstones, smashed two bones in her leg. After another big operation, she suffered, immobile, for months. My husband John and I had booked two much-needed weeks with a Christian holiday company in Turkey that June. By the third day there, I'd managed to relax and have some great times with God, but on the fourth day John was suddenly taken ill. I found myself sitting dazed alongside the ambulance driver who was taking my husband I knew not where, down terrible bumpy roads.

I've noted that the Psalms often describe God lifting the psalmist up but they don't mention the part played by the prayers of other believers. While John spent 28 hours in a wonderful Turkish hospital, all the Richmond Holidays staff and guests interceded. Once briefed by email, our home church joined in. John knew supernatural peace. Surprisingly, I didn't resent the curtailment of that much-needed holiday and felt far less shaky than I'd have expected. The practical support on all fronts was amazing, too.

When the immediate emergency passed, we were flown home, whereupon John started writing worship songs—two in a couple of weeks. We were able to thank everyone for their prayers and to lift God up by 'proclaiming his saving acts'—if not 'in the great assembly', at least to our church and Richmond Holidays, and now in these notes. I pray that 'many will see and put their trust in him'.

Lord, I'm so grateful that, with you, no one ever travels alone. You lift us out of some very sticky situations to praise you.

CHRIS LEONARD

Lifting our souls

Let the morning bring me word of your unfailing love, for I have put my trust in you. Show me the way I should go, for to you I lift up my soul. Rescue me from my enemies, O Lord, for I hide myself in you.

After the euphoria of John's dramatic rescue from medical emergency in Turkey, mini-crises continued for months, always at night or weekends. Every time, I felt responsible yet helpless, and continued stress and worry began to wear me down. I found help through the Psalms.

David suffered a longer and far worse series of emergencies—battles with himself, with his family and with enemies among his own and foreign peoples. He kept lifting to the Lord his soul, eyes, hands, voice and head—even 'our banners in the name of our God' (Psalm 20:5). He often 'exalted' (lifted up) God in praise. So it's not just God who lifts us: we have a part to play, too. In many psalms we can see huge change taking place—a surge of faith and confidence—after David 'lifts' his eyes or soul to God. The crisis may remain but he has raised his focus to God's love and power.

How? Psalm 143 says it (nearly) all. Pray, according to God's will and nature. Ask for mercy, not 'fairness'. Tell it like it is: be honest, not breezily 'super-spiritual': David was 'crushed' and 'in darkness', his heart 'dismayed', his spirit 'faint' within him. Remember then what God has done in the past: so many psalms list God's mighty deeds on behalf of David and his ancestors. Thank him. Spread out your hands ready to receive his goodness. Tell him you need him, desperately. Ask him to show you his will and the way to go: it's often not knowing what to do for the best that's most stressful. Pray in his name, for his glory and plans before your own. Ask him to silence and destroy his and your enemies, including internal ones, like worry and inconsistency of trust in him.

Lord, it's easy to say I trust in you in happy times. Help me to keep lifting my soul, my vulnerable being, to trust you when all seems amiss. Thank you for saving David's soul—and ours.

CHRIS LEONARD

Lifted through portals of praise

Lift up your heads, you gates; be lifted up, you ancient doors, that the King of glory may come in. Who is this King of glory? The Lord, strong and mighty.

Psalm 24 describes the festal procession bringing the ark of the covenant up to the tabernacle in Jerusalem. That ark, filled with God's special holy presence, had proved powerfully dangerous. Those coming near without 'clean hands and a pure heart' might die. We Christians, though, live under the new covenant deal sealed by Jesus' death and resurrection. If we believe in him and repent, we've put on his holiness in God's sight and have no more need to fear.

I'm excited to have discovered something I never knew before about this psalm. The Hebrew word rendered 'doors' means 'openings' or 'portals', while 'ancient' denotes the vanishing point of time. So here are portals to eternity—or, as Jesus put it, to 'eternal life' or 'life in all its fullness' (John 10:10). Christians receive eternal life through faith in Jesus. We live both in his eternal dimension and in this time–space world, where we, lifted and opened to him, serve as portals enabling his presence to be more fully felt. Just as Jesus did during his time on earth, we make the invisible visible. 1 Peter 2:5 says, 'You also, like living stones, are being built into a spiritual house.' Our lives, our worship, make manifest his presence on earth.

Entering into praise often lifts us closer to him. When I'm down, exhausted and feeling utterly unspiritual, I can't chirp about loving God more and more each day, but I am so grateful for the songs and hymns that express eternal truths about him. Singing them when we're alone can become a portal, raising us to that heavenly dimension. This is even better done with others: when my mother lay dying, she and I sang 'In heavenly love abiding' together, making a terrible noise but finding such balm and blessing in that thinnest of places between time and eternity.

'Enter his gates with thanksgiving and his courts with praise; give thanks to him and praise his name. For the Lord is good and his love endures for ever; his faithfulness continues through all generations' (Psalm 100:4–5).
CHRIS LEONARD

God lifting us

Blessed are those whose help is the God of Jacob… he remains faithful for ever. He upholds the cause of the oppressed and gives food to the hungry. The Lord sets prisoners free… gives sight to the blind… lifts up those who are bowed down.

I thought I had everything sorted, through what I'd learnt from the Psalms. When troubles press in, lift your focus from them to the Lord, trust in his power and love, and thank him. It's simple—and so much better than moaning all the time.

But I've said already that these notes, like the Psalms themselves, chart a rollercoaster journey. Keeping my teaching, writing, family and church responsibilities going while a succession of worrying things happened caught up with me after two years. Exhausted, yet unable to sleep, I'd snap at John. God seemed to have disappeared. I teetered, terrified, on the edge of a dark abyss. My self—my essential, vulnerable being—seemed lost, finished. Many friends had survived far worse traumas than ours: I felt that my faith was rubbish.

All that I have written in the last two notes is true. We do have a part to play in lifting ourselves Godwards—but we're not pulling ourselves up by our own bootstraps. He is the Saviour, the one who lifts us. Jesus outlined the mission that the Father had given him as proclaiming good news to the poor, freedom for prisoners and sight for the blind and 'to set the oppressed free' (Luke 4:18–21). In Luke 5:31 he says, 'It is not the healthy who need a doctor, but those who are ill.' In other words, he is there for those who are going under, for those whose faith is 'rubbish'. He delights in saving such people.

The Psalms describe God lifting us far more often than they mention us lifting ourselves to him. He lifts the needy from the ash-heap, dust, the gates of death, depths, the miry pit and affliction. He lifts his hand, voice and horn (strength/power) on behalf of the helpless and lifts a banner for those who fear him. He exalts his people, those who walk in the light of his presence.

Thank you, Lord that we can trust you and wonder at your saving power. Thank you that you know the end from the beginning, and will never leave it too long before you rescue us.

CHRIS LEONARD

How God lifted me

Elijah was afraid and ran for his life... 'I have had enough, Lord,' he said. 'Take my life; I am no better than my ancestors.' Then he lay down under the bush and fell asleep. All at once an angel touched him and said, 'Get up and eat.'

The Psalms, I find, are not especially clear about *how* God lifts us, in practical terms. Elijah's story really helps me, though. This mighty prophet had an amazing relationship with God, who empowered him to confront some big enemies (the prophets of Baal) in his name by performing one of the greatest miracles in the Old Testament (1 Kings 18:19–46). Yet straight afterwards he ran into the desert, terrified by a queen's threat, wanting to give up and die. I'd heard a preacher say that this was a classic case of burn-out. How did God lift Elijah? He sent rest, food and drink, plus an angel with specific instructions about the way he should go. Those instructions led him not back into another confrontation with God's enemies but to a personal meeting with the Lord, who promised to provide others to work alongside him.

I'd performed no miracles and was neither a prophet nor suicidal, but my 'angel' was my honest prayer partner, who said, 'You're on the edge of burn-out, Chris. Don't be frightened, you'll be OK—but you have to stop.'

I listened, for once. I cancelled writing groups and worship leading and let the younger generation do all the catering for our big family celebration of Dad's 90th birthday. I walked the beautiful countryside with John, who was at the stage of recovery when he needed gentle exercise; it 'lifted' me, too. We booked short breaks away. Other 'angels', who didn't know the situation, sent encouragement out of the blue. Different strangers told me how some Bible reading notes I'd written had helped them. A fast-growing African church wanted to reprint my very first book, originally published in 1989. I wasn't complete rubbish, then! At last I could hear God's still small voice and sense his smile: 'Rubbish? Child, I love you!'

Thank God that he sees beauty where we see only ashes. Pray for those who have sunk to rock bottom, especially those in burn-out. It's more common than you'd think among Christians, but our God can lift us.

CHRIS LEONARD

Lifting one another

I say of the holy people who are in the land, 'They are the noble ones in whom is all my delight.'

Martin, on the leadership team of my church, was diagnosed with myeloma. Even during in-patient stints of intensive therapy, he remained quietly cheerful. Patients and staff who saw him with Bible reading notes often asked questions and he shared something of his faith with them. When not in hospital, he chaired church meetings in his usual calm, loving, efficient way. Everyone respected and loved this highly capable yet humble man. Our church members knew that we, as well as the local community and his family, would be much poorer without Martin.

My friend Jo, leading the worship one Sunday after his death, spoke of geese flying in a 'V' formation. Apart from the leading bird, each goose gains 60 per cent lift, and thus strength and endurance, from the wingbeats of those in front. 'I didn't know Martin that well,' Jo said, 'yet coming here each Sunday I was conscious of being lifted because I could see Jesus in him. I still feel that. And I'm lifted by all of you living out Jesus' life here, each according to your own personality. We're flying together. Each of us has to beat our own wings, but in doing so we help lift—and delight—each other.'

God has designed that kind of uplift into his church, if we follow his way and don't stray off on our own wild goose chases. During my shaky times I started to fear that faith just didn't work, that I couldn't 'fly'. But when I see others—often humble, undemonstrative people like Martin—just getting on with it, I know that faith in God is no myth, that 'flying' is possible. That's 'comfort' (literally 'strengthening alongside') given unconsciously, but there is also the conscious kind—Christians who pass on to others the comfort and uplift that God has given them.

'We can comfort those in any trouble with the comfort we ourselves receive from God' (2 Corinthians 1:4). Ask God to encourage you about how your words, and your living for him, lift others.

CHRIS LEONARD

Lifted through suffering

The poor will eat and be satisfied; those who seek the Lord will praise him... Future generations will be told about the Lord. They will proclaim his righteousness, declaring to a people yet unborn: he has done it!

I began these notes by writing about resurrection, but before it came the crucifixion, when Jesus quoted the opening words of this extraordinary psalm: 'My God, my God, why have you forsaken me?' Here is an agonising, first-person description of his experience on the cross: 'all my bones are out of joint' (v. 14); 'they pierce my hands and my feet' (v. 16); 'people stare and gloat over me... and cast lots for my garment' (vv. 17–18). David wrote these words 1000 years before Jesus lived on earth. In what sense did these things happen to him?

Jesus said of his forthcoming death, 'I, when I am lifted up from the earth, will draw all people to myself' (John 12:32). How can a broken man, dying in agony, be attractive? How can suffering draw people to God or raise the poor? For God's purposes to succeed worldwide, as described in Psalm 22's final verses, do all his servants need to suffer? Jesus' death was the all-sufficient sacrifice, yet Paul says, 'I want to know Christ—yes, to know the power of his resurrection and participation in his sufferings, becoming like him in his death, and so, somehow, attaining to the resurrection from the dead' (Philippians 3:10—11).

It's so counter-intuitive. I don't know why David had to suffer for years before he became king, why Jesus' agonies had to be so intense or why his followers are promised suffering, too. Why did my mum and mum-in-law have to linger on this earth, suffering, when they longed to be with Jesus? Did my experiences 'work for good', helping to conform me 'to the image of his Son' (Romans 8:28–29)? I can't see it yet, but I do know that suffering is easier to bear if we understand that God is able to turn it around, to do mighty things that not only lift up you and me but also 'people yet unborn'.

Lord, help us to understand these mysteries, especially when we are going through times of suffering. Pain hurts so much, but it hurts less when we know that you can redeem good even from our suffering.

CHRIS LEONARD

Lifted in glory

The heavens declare the glory of God; the skies proclaim the work of his hands. Day after day they pour forth speech; night after night they reveal knowledge.

There are so many more psalms we could consider—testimonies of God lifting people out of terrible poverty and oppression, or exhortations to 'be strong, take courage and wait for the Lord'. All these helped me when I was desperate, but I've chosen to end this series with Psalm 19 because it focuses on God.

Great and glorious kings don't wait for or follow their subjects: their subjects wait for and follow them. While waiting, seemingly alone, how can we be strong and let our hearts take courage? Look up at the clouds scudding across the blue dome of the sky or the expanse of the stars by night or the kaleidoscopes of dawn and sunset. God could have made our world without such extravagance—without feathers or ferns, whales or waterfalls. David addresses this song 'For the director of music'. God didn't have to make it possible for our spirits to be lifted by music, dance, poetry or laughter. Thank the God who included all of that in his plan: he's worth waiting for!

As Psalm 8:3–4 says, 'When I look at your heavens… what are human beings… that you care for them?' (NRSV). But he does care and he is good! When the news seems all bad, we can sink into the belief that nothing is good or hopeful in this world, but God's law is still 'perfect, refreshing the soul', making wise the simple, giving joy to the heart and light to the eyes (19:7–8). Paul tells us to think about whatever is noble, right, pure, lovely, excellent and praiseworthy (Philippians 4:8), here and eternally. 'For our light and momentary troubles are achieving for us an eternal glory that far outweighs them all. So we fix our eyes not on what is seen, but on what is unseen, since what is seen is temporary, but what is unseen is eternal' (2 Corinthians 4:17–18).

May these words of my mouth and this meditation of my heart be pleasing in your sight, Lord, my Rock and my Redeemer.

CHRIS LEONARD

Making links

Christine Platt writes:

Childhood should be a wonderful time of life. Many parents are shocked at how quickly the years flash by. Suddenly their baby is starting school, developing his or her own mind, and doesn't seem to need them any more. There can be a wistful looking back to the fun of early childhood days. Despite that, every wise parent wants their children to grow up, become independent and reach their full potential.

Paul wants the same for God's people. Spiritual growth starts in the mind. We have to believe right truths before we can do right actions with right motives. Just as there is no point demanding that a ten-year-old wear a cycle helmet without explaining why, it's ultimately futile to encourage young believers to live God's way without explaining the reasons. Why would they be motivated to obey God, which will involve some self-denial, if they are not convinced of his love for them and of his good plans for their lives?

Blind, unthinking obedience doesn't last the distance. Jesus spoke of seed being planted in rocky places where it springs up but quickly dies because it has no root of understanding. How many believers do you know who started their Christian walk with enthusiasm but turned aside later or remained Christians in name only, with no fruitfulness? That's a desperately sad failure of effective discipleship.

Paul spends the first three chapters of Ephesians explaining the wonders and magnificence of God's love and calling for all his people. It seems that he can't find enough superlatives to do it justice. We are chosen, adopted, loved and redeemed by the priceless blood of Christ and destined to live in unity as his body. Having laid the foundation of truth, the next three chapters explain how to live it out in a daily, practical way. Paul is determined that we don't put the cart before the horse: if we fill the mind with truth, positive actions will follow. Let Paul's words restore and renew your vision and understanding of God's special love for you and the place he has planned for you in his world. Take every opportunity to share these truths with others so that we all become like seed that produces one-hundredfold of what was planted, for the praise and honour of our Saviour.

Soar high on wings like eagles

All praise to God… who has blessed us with every spiritual blessing in the heavenly realms because we are united with Christ. Even before he made the world, God loved us and chose us in Christ to be holy and without fault in his eyes.

My mind boggles at Paul's letter to the Ephesian believers. He paints word-pictures of lofty magnificence and I find myself scrabbling around trying to see where I could possibly fit in to these scenes of glory, holiness and triumph.

Paul tells me that I have a place of privilege in God's kingdom. It's as though I have been plucked out of my mediocre life and placed in a palace, not as a servant but as a valued member of the royal family. I have access to all the benefits and privileges imaginable.

I have to ask myself the question: why are my expectations so low? Why do I grovel in the dust when I should 'soar on wings like eagles' (Isaiah 40:31)? We sometimes hear stories of extraordinarily wealthy people who choose to live like paupers: they do not enjoy their wealth. We think, 'How weird—just give me a chance to spend that money!' However, most of us probably live as spiritual paupers even though we have access to all the spiritual riches in Christ.

My standing before God is 'to be holy and without fault'. This verse in THE MESSAGE reads 'to be made whole and holy by his love'. Are you whole and holy? Our churches are full of broken people, myself included.

As we start our readings in Paul's letter, we shall find that his aim is for us to grow up into the fullness of life that Christ intends for us. This will require a radical transformation of our thought-lives. We need to believe what God thinks about us, not what we think or the enemy's whispered lies. We are blessed. We are united with Christ. We are deeply loved. We are whole and holy.

Consider learning today's verses by heart so that you will have God's truth more deeply embedded in your mind. When you are tempted to feel insecure or bad about yourself, remember who you are in Christ.

CHRISTINE PLATT

Profound prayer

I pray for you constantly, asking God, the glorious Father of our Lord Jesus Christ, to give you spiritual wisdom and insight so that you might grow in your knowledge of God. I pray that your hearts will be flooded with light.

I prayed for some friends today: 'Lord, please heal Carol, and help my sponsor children to learn well at school', but, I now realise, I didn't pray for spiritual wisdom and insight so that they could grow in their knowledge of God or that their hearts would be flooded with light. Paul's prayer is profound.

It's tempting to focus on immediate needs—a good exam result or success in a job interview—and forget the foundation of trust in God that needs to be laid. There's nothing wrong with prayer for health and well-being, as long as we also cover the bases of growing in our understanding of God the Father, Son and Holy Spirit. There's little point in having a healthy body if our minds are dull and dark so that we doubt our Saviour's love.

Some of the most radiant people I have the privilege of knowing endure years of pain. Prayers for their healing are not answered in the way they would hope, but they've experienced more of God through their pain. They've got spiritual wisdom and insight and their hearts are flooded with light.

I learned one of my deepest lessons about God's love and grace during a period of illness, when I had to return home sick from the mission field. I couldn't understand why this was happening to me. Surely I was more useful to God sharing his love and word with African students than stuck in bed in England? God whispered to my aching heart, 'You are just as precious to me lying in bed unable to work as when you are busy for me in Africa. Just rest in my love.' I'm sure some people were praying for me to have spiritual insight and wisdom to understand God's ways, and I'm so grateful.

Pray through Paul's prayer for your friends and family. Try to make this a daily or weekly habit.

CHRISTINE PLATT

Masterpieces in action

God saved you by his grace when you believed. And you can't take credit for this; it is a gift from God... For we are God's masterpiece. He has created us anew in Christ Jesus, so we can do the good things he planned for us long ago.

Man and woman were the crowning glory of God's creative energy but, in a reckless bid for independence, Adam and Eve messed it all up for the rest of us. However, God was not thwarted: he created humanity anew in Christ Jesus. In one fell swoop he undid all the damage that had been wreaked on humankind. He presents this new life to us all, not to be earned but as a free gift. It's ludicrous to think we could earn our way into the favour of an unutterably holy God, yet most of us have a sneaking belief that God is more likely to accept us if we try harder. Paul has no patience with that rubbish.

I'm reading *Sarum* by Edward Rutherfurd, a novel based on the history of the English town of Salisbury from way before Roman times. It saddens me to read how faithful believers throughout the centuries truly believed that giving money to the church or paying for a stained-glass window paved their way to paradise. It was hard luck for poor people who had no opportunity for that sort of largesse.

Grace is a slippery concept. Salvation is a gift, but God expects us to 'do the good things he planned for us'. If Christ's new life in you doesn't result in fruitful service, the validity of your salvation experience comes into question.

Every masterpiece, like you and me, has a specific role to fulfil in God's kingdom. He places each of us where our particular gifts and abilities are best suited. Some people are marvellous cooks or inspirational worship leaders. I am not, and I sometimes envy my culinary and worshipful friends, but I need to do what God has gifted me for and leave catering to the masterchefs and singing to the songbirds.

God of grace, thank you for the new life you have given to me. I wholeheartedly offer myself to do the good things you have planned for me and gifted me to do.

CHRISTINE PLATT

One big happy family

You [Gentiles] are no longer foreigners and strangers, but fellow citizens with God's people and also members of his household... And in him you too are being built together to become a dwelling in which God lives by his Spirit.

From explaining salvation in individual terms, Paul now moves on to writing about how Christ's death also brought about reconciliation between Jews and Gentiles. For many of us, this may not have a huge impact, but at the time it was a major issue. The idea that Jews and Gentiles could have equal access to God was unheard of. Jews considered themselves the chosen people, but Christ's death changed everything: 'He broke down the wall of hostility that separated us' (v. 14). The new chosen people were all those who trusted Christ, regardless of ethnicity. The idea was that all God's people would be united in one big happy household, where God was delighted to be at the head of the table.

At times, members of a household hold differing views, as do members of a church. Sometimes, it seems, we forget that God is presiding at the table. Would we really talk negatively, gossip, argue with anger or harbour bitterness if we remembered that God was listening and watching?

Some aspects of the Gentile lifestyle were offensive and incomprehensible to Jews and vice versa. They all had to work hard to establish and maintain unity and learn to disagree graciously. On occasion, we let the silliest things divide us—hymns or choruses, style of worship, the volume of the music, the Bible version we prefer or what people wear.

My hope is that when the watching world looks at Jesus' followers, they would increasingly see an expression of unity among people of different ethnicities, socio-economic backgrounds, age groups and any other sections of society that exist. Wouldn't that be marvellous? Wouldn't you love to be part of a community like that? This is what Jesus died for.

Father God, thank you for welcoming me into your household. Help me to play my part in establishing and maintaining unity in the community of believers that I'm involved with, for your glory.

CHRISTINE PLATT

The privilege of serving

By God's grace and mighty power I have been given the privilege of serving him by spreading this Good News. Though I am the least deserving of all God's people, he graciously gave me the privilege of telling the Gentiles.

Studying Paul's life can be somewhat daunting. He endured shipwrecks, floggings, being hounded by authorities and imprisonment, yet he was a tireless evangelist, constantly on the alert for opportunities to talk about Jesus.

The verse quoted above gives us two clues as to what propelled him onward, despite all obstacles. He grasped hold of God's grace and mighty power; he also passionately believed that to serve God was a huge privilege, even though he considered himself 'the least deserving of all God's people' (v. 8). He had a big view of God and a humble opinion of himself.

I am not a courageous evangelist. I live in a secular environment; opportunities to talk about spiritual matters rarely come (or maybe the truth is that I seldom notice them) and I find I'm often concerned about causing disagreements. When I was young in the faith, I was bolder and tried to argue people into the kingdom. After some bruising encounters, I became a little wiser and now aim to share my faith 'in a gentle and respectful way' (1 Peter 3:15–16).

There's a balancing act between boldness and gentleness. Sometimes, days or even weeks go by and I realise I've not shared anything with any not-yet-believer about the most significant relationship in my life or about the most important question facing humankind. Maybe the answer is to put 1 Peter 3:15–16 together with 2 Timothy 4:1–2. Because Jesus will one day return as judge, we need to 'preach the word... whether the time is favourable or not'. Isn't any sacrifice worth paying, or the risk of any potential mockery or rift in a relationship worth taking, if it means more people can hear and respond to the gospel of Jesus?

In the light of the privilege of serving God, think about your friends and family. Determine in your heart to share your faith this week and ask God for both boldness and gentleness.

CHRISTINE PLATT

All you need is love

May you experience the love of Christ, though it is too great to understand fully. Then you will be made complete with all the fullness of life and power that comes from God.

'All you need is love,' sang The Beatles, and it's true, but it has to be the real thing, not counterfeit. Christ's love alone is pure. He totally accepts the loved one and always acts in their best interests. His love is not dependent on our good behaviour, although our enjoyment of his love will be dulled by sin.

A friend of mine hates being on her own. This leads her to embark on one relationship after another. She is searching for love, but her needs, like the needs of us all, are too great for any human being to meet, so she is constantly disappointed. Christ's love alone makes us complete. With him we enjoy life to the full. We then have a deep well of love within us so that we can love others, even those we might consider unlovable.

The experience of Christ's love is not a one-off job. We need to keep growing in it. I recently had a growth moment when I was presented with an opportunity to do something I had wanted to do for years. It cost a considerable amount of money. I sensed God saying, 'Go for it!' but I hesitated. Eventually I realised that the root of my uncertainty was a fundamental disbelief that God would be kind enough to give me such a treat or thought I was worth spending so much money on. That unbelief seemed ridiculous in the light of Paul's words. Christ's love is inexhaustible and extends even to me and to you—so I repented and embraced the opportunity!

In THE MESSAGE, verse 18 reads, 'Reach out and experience the breadth! Test its length! Plumb the depths! Rise to the heights! Live full lives, full in the fullness of God.'

Loving Lord, thank you for loving me just as I am. I want to know more of your love day by day. Help me to reach out to experience the breadth, the length, the depth and the height.

CHRISTINE PLATT

Lifelong learners

[Our Christian leaders'] responsibility is to equip God's people to do his work and build up the church, the body of Christ. This will continue until we all come to such unity in our faith and knowledge of God's Son that we will be mature in the Lord.

My youngest great-nephew is learning to talk. So far, his vocabulary consists of 'car'. The whole family is delighted and eager to help him improve his communication skills, so we applaud all his efforts. God is equally or even more delighted with our progress in the faith. As my great-nephew has his family to encourage and guide him, so also God has given us helpers—our Christian leaders—to promote our maturity in him.

My great-nephew's attitude to life and learning is one of wonder and unadulterated enthusiasm. He is curious about how things work and eager to try to do things for himself, even though he still needs Mummy's help when life gets too complicated—like when his train set falls apart. Wouldn't it be wonderful if all God's people had a similar attitude to learning about God and how to build up his church—an attitude of wonder, enthusiasm, eagerness to have a go and readiness to ask for help when life gets tough?

I vividly remember the first time I was asked to speak in public about my faith. I was literally sick with fear. My mentors didn't take pity on me and let me off. They knew I needed to have a go, so they helped me prepare and prayed for me. To my amazement, some years later I found myself preaching to hundreds of people and thoroughly enjoying it. I'm so grateful for those godly people who took time to equip me to help build up the body of Christ. I haven't always shown the same eagerness to learn as my great-nephew does, but I'm working on it.

God's purpose for all of his people is continual growth—each day coming to know Jesus more deeply and becoming more equipped in our service for him.

Are you a lifelong learner or have you reached a plateau? Ask God for new experiences and new adventures with him so that you can be an increasingly effective worker in his kingdom.

CHRISTINE PLATT

Put off and put on

You were taught, with regard to your former way of life, to put off your old self... to be made new in the attitude of your minds; and to put on the new self, created to be like God in true righteousness and holiness.

Putting off an old way of life and putting on a new one implies significant action and effort. For some people the change is dramatic, like the drug addict, alcoholic or prison inmate who becomes a shining beacon for the Saviour. For most of us, the changes are perhaps more subtle but none the less noticeable to others.

Positive changes should be evident in our communication with others and in the way we spend our time, money and energy. It's incredibly sad to note that, in many countries, the divorce rate among Christians is now similar to that among non-believers. This should spur all of us on to committed prayer for Christian marriages and family life.

As we know, good outward behaviour does not always imply purity within a person. We are regularly sickened by news of Christians who have been hiding an affair or other illicit relationship, or fraud. Paul reminds us that the key to change is in our minds. What we think about will eventually lead to a certain type of behaviour. Illicit relationships, dishonesty or violent anger don't just happen; they ferment over time. If we ignore the prompting of the Holy Spirit, there will come a time when we won't even hear him calling us to account, when our conscience is hardened and we indulge in sin without the slightest sense of shame. Expressions of contrition when the sin comes to light can often convey our sadness at getting found out, not real regret.

Learning scripture and maintaining honest, accountable relationships with a few trusted friends are helpful ways of purifying our minds so that we increasingly become 'like God in true righteousness and holiness'.

'Search me, O God, and know my heart; test me and know my anxious thoughts. Point out anything in me that offends you, and lead me along the path of everlasting life' (Psalm 139:23–24).

CHRISTINE PLATT

133

Live as children of light

For you were once darkness, but now you are light in the Lord. Live as children of light (for the fruit of the light consists in all goodness, righteousness and truth) and find out what pleases the Lord.

As I write, it is the longest day of the year. I wake up to daylight and late in the evening the sun is still shining—wonderful! My roses are joyfully responding to all this light. The imagery of light and darkness follows on from yesterday's reading about putting off the old life (darkness) and putting on the new (the light of Christ)—all that is good, right and true. Light is essential for growth and Christ's light within us is essential for our new nature to blossom with goodness, righteousness and truth. When he shines his light on our ways, we find out what pleases him and also what displeases him.

As a young Christian, I struggled to love and accept one of my fellow nursing students. She irritated me immensely. I prayed and tried to like her, and one day I proudly announced to an older Christian friend that I'd succeeded in pretending to like this person for a whole day. I was chuffed with my efforts! My friend gently explained to me that I should love this girl from my heart and not just put on an act. I was deflated, but it was a good lesson for me.

I think there is a place for acting in love even when you don't feel loving, but we should not be content or self-satisfied with this state of affairs. Through my friend, God shone his light on to my shortcomings and it was an experience that I have never forgotten. I looked OK on the outside but there was no truth or goodness within. God patiently helped me. My fellow student and I never did become bosom pals but gradually there grew a greater sincerity in my attitude towards her.

Loving Lord, I want to live as a child of the light and to find out what pleases you. You know I often misunderstand and end up doing what pleases me instead. Thank you for your constant patience with me.

CHRISTINE PLATT

Rights and responsibilities

Submit to one another out of reverence for Christ… Christ is the head of the church, his body, of which he is the Saviour.

A helpful definition of 'submit' is 'to yield one's rights'. These days, we hear many strident voices demanding their rights to this, that and the other. It seems that for some people to enjoy their rights, others are obliged to forgo theirs. We hear less about the need to fulfil the responsibilities that go along with those rights, even in the most basic sense of good neighbourliness. My neighbours have the right to hold a noisy party, yet it is helpful if they give some thought to their responsibility not to make life miserable for their neighbours. Both sides need to be reasonable and willing to yield their rights. One group can celebrate—maybe not too loudly or too late—and the other group can invest in earplugs.

Christ, our Saviour, led the way in this respect. He yielded his rights to kingly privileges and lived as an obscure carpenter in a forgotten little town. Later he yielded his rights to a fair trial and suffered unjustified ill treatment and death. At any moment he could have demanded his rights but, if he had done so, world history and our future would have been catastrophically different. If Jesus, King of kings and Lord of lords, was willing to yield his rights and submit to others, how much more should we? He is our model and guide.

Some rights do need to be rigorously defended—freedom of worship, the safety of children and vulnerable adults, the equal status of women and men, and so on. Submission to one another, though, follows on from being 'filled with the Spirit' (5:18). Only with the Spirit's power and guidance will we know which rights to defend and which to yield. Usually, the most troublesome 'right' is the right to have our own way!

Lord Jesus, help me learn to submit in the right way, both in small everyday issues and major concerns. Thank you for your Holy Spirit, who will guide me in this.

CHRISTINE PLATT

The best boss

Don't just do what you have to do to get by, but work heartily, as Christ's servants doing what God wants you to do. And work with a smile on your face, always keeping in mind that no matter who happens to be giving the orders, you're really serving God.

If we have to work day after day with an irritating manager who doesn't appreciate us, it really makes a difference to remind ourselves that God is our real boss. Probably most of us have a more congenial workplace environment than that of a slave in Roman times, yet this is the person to whom Paul is writing. He urges slaves to consider their real master, not just the earthly one. We know that God has our best interests at heart, even if our earthly boss is not so magnanimous.

Roman slaves had no rights and couldn't change jobs in the hope of a better life, whereas we can look around for something that fits our talents and experience. Even so, we need to trust that we are doing the job God wants us to do, until he moves us on. Therefore it is wisest to surrender to his will with a smile on our face, rather than moping or moaning.

Even on the domestic scene, if I remind myself that I'm cleaning the windows for God, it changes my mood. Sadly, I often forget and grudgingly get the job done as quickly as possible: there's certainly no smile or enjoyment in the task.

God is just as interested in our work, whether at home or outside, as he is in our Christian service. For him there is no divide between the secular and the sacred. Every aspect of life is infused with himself. That gives us every reason to work enthusiastically and with a smile.

When asked about her work with the destitute and dying, Mother Teresa said that when she washed the ravaged bodies of the sick, she imagined that it was Christ's broken body she was caring for.

Think about your job, whether at home or outside. Find ways to remind yourself that God is your boss—maybe a specific prayer each morning or a note on your desk or in the car.

CHRISTINE PLATT

Soldiers on active duty

Finally, be strong in the Lord and in his mighty power. Put on the full armour of God, so that you can take your stand against the devil's schemes. For our struggle is not against flesh and blood but against... the spiritual forces of evil.

To wrap up our readings in Ephesians, Paul points out another aspect of growing up. We are not to remain as spiritual babies; instead, we need to become effective warriors in this life-and-death battle. God has not given us an invisibility cloak: Satan knows exactly who we are and where we are. What we do have, though, is weapons. There is no need to crouch, cowering, in a corner if we take hold of the weapons and learn to use them.

Soldiers in a human battle need to know every aspect of their weaponry so that they can employ it in an instant, which takes constant practice. The analogy applies to us. Our weapons are truth, right living, peace, faith, salvation, God's word and prayer, and they also demand daily practice. In a war situation, a soldier wouldn't dream of going on patrol without protective clothing for defence and a gun for attack. Yet, are we not often oblivious to the spiritual warfare going on around us? We saunter on to the battlefield unprotected and unarmed. No wonder we become wounded and defeated.

The ultimate victory has already been won by Jesus on the cross but Satan has not yet given up. His minions remain on active duty, so we will encounter skirmishes. Satan's objective is to distract God's people and confuse those who are still seeking God.

Jesus himself used God's word as his defence and attack against Satan's temptations in the desert (Matthew 4:1–11). He said, 'It is written...' and the enemy had to slither away defeated. Do we know what is written and how to use God's word effectively? Prayer, the Bible and your obedient life will equip you superbly for the daily battles you face.

In the Messiah, in Christ, God leads us from place to place in one perpetual victory parade. Through us, he brings knowledge of Christ (2 Corinthians 2:14, The Message).

CHRISTINE PLATT

Other Christina Press titles

In His Time Eileen Gordon-Smith (£5.99)
Five missionaries and seven children are killed in a bus crash. Where is God when it hurts? 'I am different now—I no longer fear death.'

Who'd Plant a Church? Diana Archer (£5.99)
Planting an Anglican church from scratch, with a team of four—two adults and two children—is an unusual adventure even in these days. Diana Archer gives a distinctive perspective on parish life.

Pathway Through Grief edited by Jean Watson (£6.99)
Ten Christians, each bereaved, share their experience of loss. Frank and sensitive accounts offering comfort and reassurance to those recently bereaved and new insights to those involved in counselling.

God's Catalyst Rosemary Green (£8.99)
Insight, inspiration and advice for both counsellors and concerned Christians who long to be channels of God's Spirit to help those in need. A unique tool for the non-specialist counsellor.

Angels Keep Watch Carol Hathorne (£5.99)
After 40 years, Carol Hathorne obeyed God's call to Kenya. She came face to face with dangers, hardships and poverty, but experienced the joy of learning that Christianity is still growing in God's world.

Not a Super-Saint Liz Hansford (£6.99)
Describes the outlandish situations that arise in the Manse, where life is both fraught and tremendous fun. A book for the ordinary Christian who feels they must be the only one who hasn't quite got it together.

The Addiction of a Busy Life Edward England (£5.99)
Twelve lessons from a devastating heart attack. Edward, a giant of Christian publishing in the UK, and founder of Christina Press, shares what the Lord taught him when his life nearly came to an abrupt end.

Life Path Luci Shaw (£5.99)
Keeping a journal can enrich life as we live it, and bring it all back later. Luci Shaw shows how a journal can also help us grow in our walk with God.

Other BRF titles

Reflecting the Glory   Tom Wright (£8.99)
You can't love an abstraction. You can't even love the idea of love. You can only truly love a person. The relevance of knowing God in Jesus is that when we love God in Jesus we discover how that love, that personal love, is given to us in order that it may be given through us. BRF's Lent book for 2015 explores how we reveal Jesus even at the lowest and weakest points of our lives. Drawing on New Testament passages, with a particular focus on Paul's letters to the church in Corinth, Tom Wright shows that through God's Holy Spirit, the suffering but also the glory of Christ can be incarnate in our lives, enabling us to be the people of God for the world.

Walking with Old Testament Women   Fiona Stratta (£8.99)
Walking with Old Testament Women follows the same imaginative, Ignatian-style approach as Fiona Stratta's well-received first book, *Walking with Gospel Women*. Taking twelve women characters, some familiar, some less-known, Fiona uses monologues and reflective questions to explore what their experiences can teach us today. Suitable for both group and individual use, the book offers a gentle introduction for those who have not encountered the stories before, but can also be a refreshing resource for those who feel they know the stories well.

Living Liturgies   Caroline George (£7.99)
This book offers a creative worship resource for pastoral ministry with those at an often overlooked time of life—the move from independent living to dependency, or from the 'third age' to the 'fourth age' of life. The twelve liturgies—and accompanying reflections for those leading the worship—were developed by Caroline George after many years of working in church and community settings with older people. Each specially written liturgy uses a simple structure based around a theme to weave together experience, scripture and the assurance of God's love and grace. Conversation is used to connect the theme with past, present and future, leading into prayer and silent reflection with the help of a visual aid.

The Act of Prayer   John Birch (£7.99)
The Act of Prayer is a comprehensive volume of contemporary prayers based on themes arising from the *Common Worship* lectionary, the three-year cycle of Bible readings followed by many churches. Each set of prayers comprises an opening petition plus prayers of adoration, confession and thanksgiving for each of the Sundays in the church calendar plus extra festival days.

YOU CAN ORDER THE TITLES ON THESE TWO PAGES FROM CHRISTINA PRESS OR BRF, USING THE ORDER FORMS ON PAGES 140 AND 141.

Christina Press Publications Order Form

All of these publications are available from Christian bookshops everywhere or, in case of difficulty, direct from the publisher. Please make your selection below, complete the payment details and send your order with payment as appropriate to:

Christina Press Ltd, 17 Church Road, Tunbridge Wells, Kent TN1 1LG

		Qty	Price	Total
8700	God's Catalyst	___	£8.99	___
8701	Women Celebrating Faith	___	£5.99	___
8702	Precious to God	___	£5.99	___
8703	Angels Keep Watch	___	£5.99	___
8704	Life Path	___	£5.99	___
8705	Pathway Through Grief	___	£6.99	___
8706	Who'd Plant a Church?	___	£5.99	___
8707	Dear God, It's Me and It's Urgent	___	£6.99	___
8708	Not a Super-Saint	___	£6.99	___
8709	The Addiction of a Busy Life	___	£5.99	___
8710	In His Time	___	£5.99	___

POSTAGE AND PACKING CHARGES				
	UK	Europe	Surface	Air Mail
£7.00 & under	£1.25	£3.00	£3.50	£5.50
£7.01–£29.99	£2.25	£5.50	£6.50	£10.00
£30.00 & over	free	prices on request		

Total cost of books   £ ___
Postage and Packing   £ ___
TOTAL   £ ___

All prices are correct at time of going to press, are subject to the prevailing rate of VAT and may be subject to change without prior warning.

Name _____

Address _____

_____

_____ Postcode _____

Telephone number _____

Total enclosed £ _____ (cheques should be made payable to 'Christina Press Ltd')

❏ Please do not send me further information about Christina Press publications

DBDWG0115